W9-BJR-795

THE LIBRARY ENVIRONMENT / ASPECTS OF INTERIOR PLANNING

The Library Environment

Aspects of Interior Planning

Proceedings of the

LIBRARY EQUIPMENT INSTITUTE

Conducted at St. Louis, Missouri,

June 26-27, 1964

Sponsored by the

Library Administration Division

American Library Association

Edited by Frazer G. Poole

AMERICAN LIBRARY ASSOCIATION

Chicago, 1965

Copyright © 1965 by the American Library Association

Manufactured in the United States of America

Library of Congress Catalog Card Number 65-24956

Cover photograph:
Informal area
Charles Leaming Tutt Library
Colorado College
Colorado Springs, Colorado

Foreword

The second Institute on Library Equipment, sponsored by the Equipment Committee of the Library Administration Division, American Library Association, was held June 26-27, 1964, at the Coronado Hotel, St. Louis, Missouri. As in the earlier Institute (University of Miami, 1962), the emphasis was primarily on library furnishings and equipment rather than on building planning.

More than five hundred librarians, trustees, architects, consultants, representatives of manufacturers supplying equipment to the profession, and others attended and participated in the discussions that followed presentation of the formal papers.

Members of the Section on Buildings and Equipment who assisted in planning the Institute and who served as moderators of the several panel discussions were: William S. Geller, chairman, Equipment Committee; Frank E. Gibson, chairman, Section on Buildings and Equipment; and Frazer G. Poole. To Mr. Roderick Swartz, Assistant to the Executive Secretary of the Library Administration Division, and other members of the Division staff are due the thanks of the Equipment Committee for the excellent hotel arrangements and for the efficient handling of matters relating to advance planning, registration, and finances. Grateful appreciation is also due Dr. Andrew J. Eaton, Director of the Washington University Libraries, and Dr. James V. Jones, Director of the St. Louis University Libraries, for the receptions and tours of their respective libraries, which they hosted on successive nights following conclusion of the evening programs.

This report includes the texts of the papers given at the Institute, as well as the presentations of the panelists and the discussions that ensued between members of the audience and the program speakers. Unfortunately, the discussion that followed the paper on "Lighting the Library: Standards for Illumination," by Dr. H. Richard Blackwell, was not recorded and therefore was not available for inclusion in these Proceedings.

In some instances the speakers used slides to illustrate their talks. Diagrams and similarly important illustrative materials are reproduced in the Proceedings, but it was not feasible to reproduce the many colored slides of buildings and other general subjects.

ALPHONSE F. TREZZA
Executive Secretary
Library Administration Division

AMERICAN LIBRARY ASSOCIATION

Library Administration Division

Section on Buildings and Equipment
    Frank E. Gibson, *Chairman*
        Director
        Omaha Public Library
        Omaha, Nebraska
    Howard M. Rowe, *Vice-Chairman*
        Chief Librarian
        Free Public Library
        San Bernardino, California
    Marylyn Davis, *Secretary*
        Librarian
        Pennsbury High School Library
        Yardley, Bucks County
        Pennsylvania

Committees
Architecture Committee for Public Libraries
    A. Chapman Parsons, *Chairman*
        Librarian
        Alliance Public Library
        Alliance, Ohio
Buildings Committee for College and University Libraries
    Richard A. Farley, *Chairman*
        Director of Libraries
        Kansas State Teachers College
        Emporia, Kansas
Buildings Committee for Hospital and Institution Libraries
    Mrs. Elsa Freeman, *Chairman*
        Librarian
        U.S. Housing and Home Finance Agency
        Washington, D.C.
Equipment Committee
    William S. Geller, *Chairman*
        Librarian
        Los Angeles County Public Library
        Los Angeles, California
Planning School Library Quarters Committee
    Richard L. Darling, *Chairman*
        School Library Specialist
        Library Services Branch
        U.S. Office of Education
        Washington, D.C.

    Alphonse F. Trezza, *Executive Secretary*
    Roderick G. Swartz, *Assistant to the Executive Secretary*

Contents

FURNISHINGS   Informal Furnishings for the Library
   Walter A. Netsch, Jr.   9
Design and Construction of Informal
Furnishings—A Panel Discussion
   Vincent Cafiero   12
   James Lucas   13
   Jens Risom   15
   Martin Van Buren   17
   Discussion   17

ILLUMINATION   Lighting the Library—Standards
for Illumination
   H. Richard Blackwell   23
Principles of Illumination for Libraries
   Brock Arms   32

AUDIO   Listening Facilities in the Library
   C. Walter Stone   34
Audio Services and Facilities—
A Panel Discussion
   Stephen Ford   41
   Philip Lewis   42
   Wendell W. Simons   44
   Discussion   48

TRANSPORTATION   Transporting Books and People in the
Library
   Keyes D. Metcalf   51
   Discussion   55

FLOORING   The Carpeted Library
   Joe B. Garrett   57
Resilient Flooring Materials in Libraries
   George F. Johnston   60
Flooring Materials for Libraries—
A Panel Discussion
   Charles Dalrymple   64
   Homer L. Fletcher   64
   Alfred Rawlinson   65
   Joan Shinew   67
   Discussion   68

Informal Furnishings for the Library

WALTER A. NETSCH, JR.
A.I.A.
Skidmore, Owings, and Merrill
Chicago, Illinois

Informal furnishings have been a greatly used, and often misused, feature of the library environment. The trend toward informality in furnishings in today's library reflects a trend toward lack of ceremony in our approach to serious pursuits. Formerly reading rooms were massive and extremely formal in design, necessitating some small informal area to retreat to for occasional relaxation. Today, this is not the case. The retreat is no longer necessary. The planning of informal furnishings now relates to the total complex of each library's design.

We are all aware of the different types of libraries: the small community public library, the large public library, the high school library, the college and university library, the undergraduate library, the research library, the information center, the industrial library. There are also differences in library patrons, and we are gradually learning to recognize these differences and their significance in terms of patron needs.

Within each of these types of libraries recognition must be given to various reader demands and the manner in which general services, such as bibliographic and reference materials, periodicals, the browsing collection, and the general book collection, are handled. Special elements, such as the audiovisual department, special or rare book collections, poetry and reading rooms, lounges, typing rooms, and the like include informal reading activities in which the character of the seating space is related to specific functions.

The group study room is a new and important example of specialized informal reader space. Psychologically and physiologically, the use and disposition of informal furnishings here develop new demands, as sociological habits in the needs of readers are recognized. Edward T. Hall, social-anthropologist at the Illinois Institute of Technology, in *The Silent Language*[1] and also in his later works, reaffirms this problem for architects and others in-

volved in the disposition of the environment when he discusses the habits of communication and the area of influence that the individual selects as his domain in relation to his neighbor.

We all know that the sofa has not been successful as a panacea for all the problems involved in planning informal furnishings. Along with the sofa, the often-used three or four chairs about a coffee table is a habitually misused environmental arrangement. The grouping, when analyzed, is shown to derive from living-room furniture patterns, in which oral communication is encouraged. Such patterns are hardly appropriate for the library. Another common failing is that, too often, informal furnishings have been placed at that point in the library where nothing else will fit.

According to Webster, "informal" means: "(a) not in accord with prescribed or fixed customs, rules, ceremonies, etc.," or "(b) casual, easy, unceremonious, or relaxed." This definition of "informal," when applied to furnishings in a library, must be related to a knowledge of the purposes of the various areas within the library and which of these purposes might appropriately be pursued in an atmosphere which is "casual, easy, unceremonious, or relaxed."

With the continuing emphasis on the importance of the individual reader and the individual environment, the informal or easy aspect of library furniture arrangement must limit rather than encourage oral communication, wherever quiet is required. At the same time, the informal arrangement must limit the amount of neighborly disturbance that nonfixed seating may help to create. We need, therefore, to develop designs for informal seating that provide comfort without encouraging oral communication. Such designs should make possible a variety of postures and uses within that area of the library in which the individual's needs are best satisfied.

Libraries we have designed include the Skokie Public Library, the Grinnell College Library, the Colorado College Library, the John Crerar Library at the Illinois Institute of Technology, and the Air Force Academy Library at Colorado Springs. Only use will reveal how successful some of our furniture designs are, but clearly there are still opportunities to develop better informal furnishings for the library. In exploring these opportunities, several factors in the changing pattern of library use should be considered.

First, recognition should be given to the more serious use of libraries resulting from Sputnik and the "knowledge explosion." People are increasingly aware that only through education can they find their places in the new scientific society. Recognition

1. Edward T. Hall, *The Silent Language* (Garden City, N.Y.: Doubleday, 1959).

should be given, also, to the changes in cultural patterns occurring in our society. When I was in school, for example, a white shirt, a tie, and a coat were essential. Today, whether one walks into a public library or into a college or university library, casual attire is the accepted mode of dress. This change in dress habits is simply a visual reflection of the total cultural change to more informal living. Finally, consideration should be given to the many new materials available: for example, carpeting used not only as a surface on which to walk but also on which to sit, as the thickly padded carpet and cushions of the children's reading area at the Skokie Public Library. With these criteria, and with recognition of the types of communications required in libraries, new attitudes can be developed toward seating.

A major consideration in the development of informal seating is the need to perfect coordinated designs for new families of furniture that will recognize these different demands, rather than to accept, as we now do, a random selection of individual items. Furniture for individual seating, aside from the carrel, must be serviceable, practical, and adapted to a variety of physical attitudes and activities. It should imply use for casual, easy, unceremonious, relaxed study.

We must also recognize that aside from the special elements of the library that have replaced the scattered informal spaces formerly considered essential, more of the demands for informal reading facilities are being accommodated in group study areas. These provide for the oral communication and unregimented action that are facets of the educational process in a contemporary library.

Here are a few suggestions for furniture to be used in informal reading areas which the panelists may want to discuss. The items suggested can provide for a variety of postures and uses. First and simplest (and least flexible for other uses) is the low-back, upholstered, side-arm chair which permits a variety of informal postures for reading when taking notes is not required. A variant of the same unit, installed in small groups, with a collapsible tablet arm added, gives an opportunity for either informal lounge-type reading or carrel-type reading.

The third solution is a high-backed, oversized, tablet-arm chair such as our forefathers once used. Many of you have seen chairs like this that were used by Franklin, Adams, and Jefferson. A similar chair in modern design does not resemble such chairs in detail, but the function is the same as that of the chairs used in colonial times. The high back establishes a realm of privacy, while the oversized tablet arm permits use as a carrel. The scale of the enclosure provides a variety of postures. In essence, this is an informal study carrel.

A fourth solution is the high-back chair comfortably upholstered, such as a Saarinen chair, the

Eames chair, or the Bertoia high-back chair. Each of these, of course, requires a footstool. Fifth and last of possible solutions to the need for better informal seating is the exedra, or sculptured floor plan, which establishes seating without furnishings. Such a solution serves only for those areas in which a high degree of informality can be developed. One variant of this we have already discussed in the heavy carpet and cushions of the children's area at the Skokie Public Library. The exedra is, in essence, the adult variant and recognizes the differences in height between adult and child.

No sofas have been included in this list because the overly relaxed attitude of reading while lying down seems inappropriate to the library environment. Moreover, it is, as we all know, a good way to have one reader occupy space that is designed for two or three.

In placing items of informal furniture, quantity becomes important. Too many pieces give the impression of a railroad station. Arrangements of furniture should avoid groupings containing too many pieces, as well as groupings encouraging oral communication. Several effective possible furniture patterns include:

Pinwheel

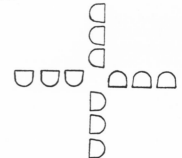

Short Chain (in which the direction of the reader is varied)

Linear (in which a variety of spaces is utilized)

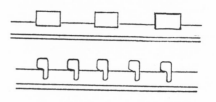

Exedra

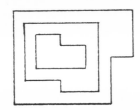

Informal reading or study arrangements must, of course, recognize the need for enclosed group study areas containing tables and chairs as well as blackboard and electrical outlet for typewriters; or chairs only, with or without a collapsible tablet arm, plus a blackboard, typing stand, and electrical outlet.

In conclusion, I think the following assumptions can be made:

The need for informal seating lessens with the rising demand for individual seating in the library

The quality of informal seating should be related to a composite of library use and cultural attitudes

Informal seating should provide for a variety of postures

There is a need, if these seating types are to be developed, for a coordinated group or groups of furniture designs which would be aesthetically more pleasing in the library than many individual designs now in use

The flexibility and movability of some informal seating must be considered, and patterns should be developed strong enough to keep a semblance of order

There must be recognition that some of these informal furnishings will cost more than the carrel and chair otherwise provided

In special areas, in which the primacy of study or research reading is not so demanding, sofas can be used

Design and Construction of Informal Furnishings— A Panel Discussion

Moderator:
　WILLIAM S. GELLER
　Librarian
　Los Angeles County Public Library
　Los Angeles, California

Panel Members:
　VINCENT CAFIERO
　Designer
　Knoll Associates, Inc.
　New York City, New York

　JAMES LUCAS
　Director of Public Relations
　Herman Miller, Inc.
　Zeeland, Michigan

　JENS RISOM
　Jens Risom Design, Inc.
　New York City, New York

　MARTIN VAN BUREN
　Interior Planning Consultant
　Charlotte, North Carolina

VINCENT CAFIERO

Before we take up the matter of furniture and furnishings, I should like to start with a discussion of architecture. As has been mentioned, there is absolutely no doubt about the relationship between good furnishings—that is, furnishings appropriate for a particular use at a particular time—and their use in a particular building.

We have heard, earlier in the program, about a number of new social developments, especially the informality and the lack of discipline shown by some of our young people. This is probably our own fault because it is the way we, ourselves, live.

Technically, we have moved very rapidly in a very short period of time. We have learned the technology of construction so that we can design a building able to stand up in a swamp or withstand an earthquake, but we have not always understood the value of a well-designed building.

The importance of adequate lighting, the need for a proper functional plan for a building, the effect that a well-designed building will have on the people who work within that space, are all recognized in buildings designed for banks and insurance companies and in similar commercial structures. We

have been less successful in the building of libraries. It is unfortunate that in many instances our only concern in building a library is to develop space that will house the books. Then, at the last minute, we say: Well, we do need furniture to go into this building, so let us see what furniture is available. Too often there is not enough coordinated planning in the utilization of space and the design of the building. Space planning and building planning ought to proceed hand in hand.

Another problem created by technology and the speed with which its improvements are coming upon us, is that the library building we have today may be almost obsolete five to ten years from now. Thus it is important for us to study our changing requirements, so that we design buildings that are not only up to date the day we move in, but are up to date, usable, and workable in the future.

Furnishings for a library definitely should be designed for the building in which they will be used. They must be coordinated with the building proper. In a well-designed, properly planned building, a relationship must exist between all the elements that make up the space: the structure, the lighting, the air-conditioning system, the mechanical equipment, right down to the furnishings themselves.

One point that I would like to emphasize here relates to furnishings. All too often, as I have said, the furnishings of the library tend to be considered last, at the time when there is little money left to buy any. As a consequence, furniture is often specified that is not really appropriate for the building. I am not saying that the furniture will fall apart, but visually and from the standpoint of comfort it often is not up to par. The furnishings should be taken into account in the preliminary stages and design of the library.

I would like to tell you something about the type of work we do and the directions we have been following. We have found it almost impossible to develop a standard line of library furniture. Instead, we have created basic designs that are readily adaptable to the different requirements of different libraries. Such adaptation originates with the architect and the library building committee. In some cases, we are called in to design the library furnishings at the start of the project. In such instances we begin, with the actual design of equipment, to complement the building on the architect's drawing board.

The main charging desk for a library built recently in Yonkers, New York, was designed by us as a modular system. The counter was completely coordinated and designed to function without considerable equipment piled on top. The card trays were built into the counter. We are able to modify our desks to meet different requirements in different buildings. In another instance we combined the functions of both bookshelf and reading unit. The variations of design are many since the basic system is adaptable to many conditions.

Because of the changing functions of the library, we are becoming more involved in the areas of communication. Thus, in one library a special unit was designed for the storage of phonograph records. In this same area of the library, space was provided for the playing of these records under controlled conditions. Small reading tables in the children's section of another library were custom designed, together with low stools scaled for the children who were to use the tables.

The Connecticut General Life Insurance Company in Hartford, Connecticut, is both an employee and a research library, but it has many characteristics that can be incorporated into a public school library. In this building we used low planter units to divide seating areas or to define different sections. Earphones are built into the cabinetry so that records can be played and people listen in privacy without disturbing others around them.

The library of the Rockefeller Institute, where we had a completely different set of circumstances and environment, required rather lush treatment with soft, upholstered furniture and heavy carpeting on the floor. Much can be done to help create the proper environment in buildings, and in libraries in particular, if the design of these spaces is handled as a complete entity from the very beginning.

In the development of office space for individuals, we have taken people who have worked in old, dilapidated buildings and put them into new, well-designed ones. The effect such a change has had on the individuals is remarkable. Secretaries became more concerned with their personal appearance and grooming. The standard of dress, too, was changed. One could actually see that the environment created was having a tangible effect on the people working in that space. This effect is one we are not too familiar with, because much of the space in the buildings in which we have to work and live is uninspired or belongs to a completely different time and period. We have the technology and the ability today to make space more livable and more functional. What we lack is an understanding of what we have available and what we can do with it.

JAMES LUCAS

It seems to me that two unspoken questions are implied in the title of our topic: (1) What is the range of furniture design available today for library lounge areas? (2) What is the direction furniture design of the future will take in relation to the emerging need for library lounge areas? I would like to explore the second of these two questions.

Interior design, unlike painting, sculpture, music, drama, and literature, is a captive art. As architecture goes—that is, as the prevailing philosophies of our great architects go—so goes the interior design of our time. Everyone agrees that the interior design of a building ought to complement the exterior design. The two must be compatible.

Furniture design tends to follow the needs uncovered by the architect and, often, by the interior designer. It seems logical to assume, then, that we can get a fairly accurate picture of what direction future furniture design will take by studying existing and proposed buildings designed by such men as Walter A. Netsch, Jr., and other of our leading architects.

While furniture technology is by no means so advanced as many other technologies, furniture manufacturers are quite at home with a broad range of materials and construction techniques. We have learned how to use wood, steel, glass, aluminum, fabric, and plastic with a remarkable degree of sophistication. From this point on, our industry shares an ailment peculiar to twentieth-century man. We have considerable know-how, but very little know-what. We can produce almost anything the market needs, but what does it need?

The architect, the interior designer, and the furniture designer work to uncover and answer the needs of the client. We can all benefit by more active participation by the client in carefully articulating his present and future needs as they relate to his interior furnishings. As we work together in these matters, we begin to fill in the gap of know-what.

In this context it is interesting to think about pioneer man as compared to modern man. No one had to explain architecture or furniture design to pioneer man because he created it. He protected his family against the elements and the Indians, then proceeded to build his own home and furniture and in leisure hours create folk art and music all his own. He felt very much at one with his environment, he understood it: no one had to explain it to him because he made it.

Today in our homes and offices we are surrounded with machinery we do not understand. In my home, if the electric broom gets out of order, all is chaos; so, too, if the dishwasher fails to work. Modern man is surrounded—in fact, drowned—by technology. He feels cut off from his environment because he no longer has a hand in shaping it as he did at one time.

The question is: is it possible to furnish a library with such sensitivity to the uses of space as to encourage the people who use the space to become more selective in choosing the things with which they surround themselves in everyday life? We no longer go to the forest and cut down logs to build our own log cabin and furniture. We can, however, fashion our own environment, not by reading and believing the advertisements, but by being selective in the things we choose to live with.

We are beginning to discover that many of our ideas about what constitutes comfort are really quite relative. Libraries across the country are full of data on just what it takes to make a comfortable chair, and yet we are all aware of the fact that at a rodeo one can be quite comfortable, for maybe two hours, on a quarter of an inch of wooden rail, on top of a fence. This is a special kind of comfort. It may not suit me, but another may find it adequate. This fact implies that the importance of the moment overrides any kind of personal discomfort. It is possible to lull people to sleep in a library, as you well know.

Two words that I feel are often confused are "comfort" and "luxury." George Nelson, our chief designer, has helped to clear away some of the confusion. In telling about a trip he made to Japan several years ago, he describes one incident as a very luxurious experience. On a winter day, at a dinner in a Japanese restaurant, he sat on the bare earth. There was no central heating in the restaurant, and he kept warm by running his hands over a pot of fire beside his main dish. He found this a "luxurious" experience as compared to the "comfortable" experience of eating at a New York restaurant, where he came out feeling as overstuffed as the chair he sat on. The point is that luxury, in this case, was the feeling of oneness with nature: really feeling or tasting the food, feeling the environment, being a part of it.

Max Frisch, the Swiss author, says the same thing in a different way when he defines "technology." He suggests that technology is the ability of so arranging the world that one no longer has to experience it—an interesting way to look at the subject!

We talk glibly of the personal consequences of architecture, but just what *are* the personal consequences? What happens to the client after the building is up, the honeymoon is over, and the architect's fee has been paid? What happens in the space? In what ways are people affected by the organization of the interior spaces? It is possible to plan a building to encourage intellectual interaction. The University of Michigan has an interesting arrangement in its departments of mathematics and psychology. The departments are in two separate buildings but are linked by a passageway—an accidental feature added as an afterthought. This passageway leads to some interesting experiments in both fields of knowledge.

Some of the psychologists on the campus report, "Now we get together with the mathematicians on coffee breaks, and we conduct some interdisciplinary experiments together." Such experiments could not have happened without this accidental interaction. The point is—is it possible to leave slack in a plan? Can you foresee what kind of interaction you might wish to have in this interspace and then facilitate it?

How do people really settle into a space? How do people really *use* space?

Sometimes designs of space or furnishings backfire; people in actuality use space in a different way from that which the designers planned. We know that people tend to engineer their own privacy in lounge or other areas. Thus, they will almost invariably attempt, by adding pillows or something else, to achieve a high back to a chair if it has a low back. How can you take these needs into account in your own plans?

Another sidelight, one that is most significant, has to do with a dormitory built about six years ago. This dormitory was hailed, upon its completion, as one of the finest dormitories in the country, for it was designed by an internationally known architect. The only problem was that, after six months in the building, nearly all the residents wanted to leave. They did not want to live in the space. The university had a requirement that all the girls had to live in this building their first year on campus. After this they could move to any place they chose. Most of the girls wanted to move out after the first six months.

So the sociologist on the campus decided to investigate, and he discovered that the girls could not impress themselves on their space. All the dormitory walls were cement block. As you know, it is a little hard to argue with cement block; you can't put anything on the walls. The building was architecturally excellent, but it failed in this human relations aspect. Most of the girls preferred an old 1890 Gothic mansion with cracks in the walls and wooden floors.

Well, the sociologist went a step further and decided to interview the girls who elected to remain in the new building. Please remember this building was as *avant-garde* as any dormitory of its time. It was not a slapdash design but was the result of good, competent planning. Almost without exception, the girls living in this piece of *avant-garde* architecture had average grades and held conventional views on politics and other subjects. It was the "swingers" who had moved over to the 1890 mansion. So it turned out that all the aqualungs and the Austin-Healeys were parked in front of the old building, and all the Edsels were parked in front of the new building.

Edward Hall, in his book *The Silent Language*,[1] discusses the concept of territory. Other psychologists have discussed the same subject. In this matter we know more about animals than we do about people. A week ago in St. Louis, the American Institute of Architects held its annual convention, and one of the speakers talked about how we

1. Edward T. Hall, *The Silent Language* (Garden City, N.Y.: Doubleday, 1959).

pay more attention to designing good zoos than we do to designing good houses. This is because animals are very costly—well, have you priced polar bears lately?

In my own town we are trying to buy an elephant; we do not have one in Grand Rapids. I do not mean that Grand Rapids is a Democratic town, but we do not have an elephant and we are trying to buy one. When we do, we will take good care of that elephant, and his environment—how he relates to his living space—will be uppermost in our minds.

That was the point the speaker was making. If the spaces are not right, the animals become ill, whereas man, through the centuries, has learned to endure mediocre architecture and to adapt himself to almost anything. He can live in a coffee can if he has to. Animals have a flight distance, and we must remember that people have, too.

You might make this experiment after the meeting today. On second thought I recommend it after the cocktail hour tonight. As you are talking to someone, take a step or two back, and you will find he will follow you. Do not increase the volume of your voice; just talk normally and step back, and the person will follow. After he is advancing toward you, stop and talk a little longer, then start to walk toward him. He will back up. There is a sort of no man's land that we attempt to keep around ourselves.

Hall and others also talk about "personal space," that is, our body and its territory, which is space somewhere outside the body. Again, it is easier to analyze the situation with an animal. If two gorillas are put into a cage, one will invariably attempt to stake out the boundaries of his territory. He will take a banana peel, or whatever he has, and mark out his territory so that if another animal steps in, he can either fight or retreat.

What are our territories? Strange to say, the answer to this question brings us into furniture design. A number of years ago a great argument arose at one of the foreign ministers' meetings over the shape of the tables. Were they to be round or square? The United States wanted round tables, and Russia wanted square tables. The reason for this, one sociologist explained, was that a square table gives one an opportunity to mark off his boundaries, while a round table makes it very hard to do so. As it happens, both shapes were used, and maybe peace was given another boost; it is hard to say.

We know also that the best interaction at a board meeting takes place at the corners of the table. At a long table, with conferees all around it, the most satisfactory communication occurs at the four corners and not side to side, across the table, or down the length of the table. No one yet has explained exactly why, but this fact is true.

The psychiatrist, in an analysis, places his chair at an angle to the patient. Thus the patient has an opportunity either to look at the doctor or to look away. When the doctor gets to the part about the thumb and the blanket, the patient can look away or face him directly.

These are some of the provocative ways in which people use personal space. Can we afford to ignore them in planning the furnishings for our buildings? As if all this were not bewildering enough, I will add one more thought. There is an old saying that it is not so much what a man's environment is that is important; it is what he thinks it is. We often tend to overlook this. No matter who designs your building or who supplies your furniture, it is what the patrons inside *think* the environment is that will really have an effect on them.

We have much know-how, but we need more know-what. We need to know what to produce in order to meet your needs, and we need to know what effect our products and their use have on the psychology and sociology of people working and learning together. There is still much to be learned, but we are coming closer to defining the limits of our ignorance.

JENS RISOM

There are both advantages and disadvantages to being the third member on a panel. The advantage is that you are in a position to criticize your competitors or your friends for what they have said. The disadvantage, of course, is that they have probably already said everything you had in your notes.

In planning my remarks for today, I asked myself how we, as designers and manufacturers, could contribute to this discussion with you librarians. Perhaps the best thing for me to do is to voice a few thoughts which pertain to why we are here and how we can cope with your problems. What is our role as product people—not our company alone, but other furniture manufacturers and designers as well—in this problem of informal furnishings for libraries?

To answer this we must consider, first, the overall concept of product design—the problem of determining what it is we are trying to do, what it is we are trying to accomplish. Second, we must consider how to work together with other designers on building projects of this nature. The design and construction of informal furnishings are important, of course, not only in planning libraries but also in planning business and residential interiors.

The subject we are concerned with today is the design, construction, and selection of informal furnishings for the library. I think that what we are most concerned with, when we talk about informal furniture—I am choosing to understand the word "informal" here in its nontechnical aspect—is the act of sitting. Where do we sit down, how do we like to sit when reading, how do we like to make notes, where are we most comfortable, where are we most relaxed? All this is part of the definition of "informal furnishings," which are an aspect of relaxation. Usually we do not stand erect, or sit up straight and read, the way we were taught to do at school; these formal positions are not so effective and so appealing to us.

I like to think that although furniture is not architecture, it is perhaps the most important product helping to complete a piece of architecture. A building without furniture, even one with built-in furnishings, is an incomplete building. Obviously, we cannot visualize a library without furniture in which people can sit down. People do not just walk in, get their books, and walk out again; the function of a library is of quite a different nature.

In product design we are concerned with developing a piece of furniture that is pleasant-looking, harmonious in design, and functional. Most important, perhaps, is the proper selection of materials for the need at hand. We consider furniture as part of the building but not as part of the architecture. Too often in commercial buildings, and in libraries, too, furniture is treated as a miniature version of the building. We repeat the materials: the steel and the glass, the marble, even the concrete. This, I believe, is a mistake. Subconsciously, the occupant, the person with whom we are concerned, yearns for and needs contrasting materials.

As you probably know, most of the production of the company I represent is in wood. I do not think that people, as users of furniture, will ever learn to live without texture around them. They cannot be entirely comfortable in a room full of completely dead, hard materials. I believe, therefore, that in libraries wood is a material we should work with. We should try to work with textured floor coverings and textured materials for the furniture rather than with the impersonal, flat vinyls which are selected because they may be more practical. Buyers are often tempted to be too practical in selecting furnishings for a library, or for an office building for that matter. The proper layout and arrangement of furniture are important, too. And, finally, a psychological consideration must be given to the overall impression, the overall texture, with which we are surrounded when we use a room and especially a library, where we have to concentrate and at the same time be at ease.

The words "total design" have been used here today. Last week, in Chicago, I was fortunate to participate in a panel discussion on total design. This concept is something that may be helpful to you as clients of architects and furniture manufacturers, for it is you who will be planning your libraries and who will set the specifications and requirements. You should be extremely concerned with the necessity for total design, although it is

nothing new. It exists everywhere. Total design occurs in practically every business organization because, if it did not, the organization would fall apart. If there is a conflict between the treasurer and the sales manager, or between the production manager and the president, no one can function. Somebody has to be in charge, somebody has to set the policy, somebody has to keep the operation going.

If you set up a project for a new library and select an architect, you cannot stop there. You cannot allow the architect to begin the building, then, when you get far enough along, think of somebody who might give you advice on where the furniture goes, and then start looking around for somebody to tell you what sort of furniture you ought to have.

Instead, there should exist from the very beginning, long before the project is started, a very firm and well-considered design policy or design philosophy. For that, you need to choose a design group. This group has to function as a team, not just as a group of designers who, individually, may be excellent in their own fields. Unless their goals run in exactly the same direction and the designers fully understand how they, in their special fields, can interpret the overall design policy, you will not achieve the complete and well-planned library you have in mind.

Please remember the total-design concept. It is important to the success of your building. Too often, conflicting and unhappy results follow because a project has been undertaken without someone in charge of the total design. It seems to me that the architect, as chief designer and chief policymaker, should be the one in charge. I cannot imagine a client selecting an architect unless he has seen and is satisfied with other jobs the architect has done. If the architect's talent is best for the building, it must be best for the interior. If this system does not produce a good library, the architecture is not good. By the same token, if the furnishings are well conceived but poorly executed, they are not properly designed.

As product people, we are deeply concerned with this problem. Sometimes we are brought into the picture much too late. The ideal situation is for the architect, the landscape designer, and the interior designer to specify early the types of products and designs that are to be used throughout. If this design team is set up from the very beginning under a strong leader, then you are assured of a perfect result. I would rather see cooperative planning by mediocre designers, than a group of outstanding designers all trying to fight the battle of who is going to be first.

As furniture designers and manufacturers, we are greatly impressed with the importance of library design, with the future of library design, and with the need for well-planned furnishings for libraries. I think you will see good products from all of us within the next few years. We are aware of the problems and of the difficulties, but we need your help in clarifying the details and in outlining your requirements. In each case we need a total-design team which can work harmoniously to produce the results you want.

MARTIN VAN BUREN

I would like to speak about one particular aspect of library design, and that is comfort. Much has been said about construction and durability, about arrangement, about selection, but I believe comfort in library furniture is of the utmost importance, and I think that very little research has been done to establish the real criteria of comfort. We talk about high-back chairs, low-back chairs, wired chairs, sofas, and so forth, but how much research has been done to find out what really makes a comfortable chair?

First of all, the problem is comfort for what? Reading, talking, sleeping, relaxing? The functions for which comfort is required in libraries are, I think, clear: for reading, writing, and relaxing, yes, but certainly not for sleeping.

Let me read a statement of Lewis Mumford quoted in the *New Yorker*, October 20, 1962, concerning the library of the American Embassy in London:

"This serene library, 'all beautified with omissions,' as Henry James said of The Great Good Place, is just what a library should be—the readers' tables close to the windows, and the stacks, holding some twenty-five thousand volumes of Americana, easily accessible. To give the authentic American touch, there is even an American Bible, but no King James Version! I cannot say as much in praise of the furniture. The clumsy, armless, almost immovable chairs were obviously chosen by someone with little experience in sitting or reading, much less in note-taking; they achieve a maximum of cushioned discomfort with a minimum of efficiency, and, compared with the not altogether adequate but still commodious oak armchairs of the reading rooms in the New York Public Library at Forty-second Street, they are singularly inept. There are today, incidentally, five badly designed 'contemporary' chairs on the market for one that is even tolerably good, and the meekness with which the fashion-minded public accepts these incompetent pieces of furniture is second only to its eagerness to pay good money for the more infantile forms of modern painting. Here was a place for a dexterous innovation in modern library furniture, to match the high standard we have achieved in the conduct, if not always the design, of lending libraries."

In working on a manual of library furniture that we are doing for the Library Technology Project of the American Library Association, we have been investigating this subject for a year and a half. We have discovered very little background material of value, although we have searched the literature of this country and Europe. We have read the study on seating done by Dr. Earnest A. Hooton at Harvard in 1945,[1] and another done in 1959 at the University of Arkansas.[2] The latter work was excellent, and I would like to review briefly the methods used in the Arkansas study to show how the testing for comfort in seating was done.

To begin, three basic criteria were established: (1) basic design measurements for sitting, (2) basic types of sitting positions, and (3) basic sizes for each type of sitting position. These were then broken down into activities as follows: dining, writing, card and game playing, talking, and relaxing. Exhaustive tests were made to determine average human measurements for both men and women. For each type of activity, measurements were made of the following: overall depth of seat, depth of seat to the point of lowest depression, width of seat, height of back, width of back, slant of back, contour of back, width between armrests, height of armrests, angle of armrests, and, in addition, table heights relative to seat heights. Differences in heights and weights of both men and women were also charted.

All this sounds technical, but I want to make an important point. In trying to discover some technical data on furniture which would relate to the library, we contacted numerous manufacturers who were supposed to be leaders in the field. After a year and a half of searching, we found very little technical information that could be accepted as proven. You might call this statement a complaint. It is. It seems to me that this sort of research in the library profession is long overdue, and I hope that the manufacturers will begin to conduct such tests with results that will prove themselves in libraries and in informal seating yet to come.

Discussion

Question: Is it possible to design a building so as to encourage an intellectual interchange, as in the accidental interchange between the mathematicians and the psychologists cited by Mr. Lucas? Could he go into some detail as to adaptations of that concept in a library building?

1. Earnest A. Hooton, *A Survey in Seating, Instituted by the Heywood-Wakefield Company* (Cambridge, Mass.: Harvard Univ., Dept. of Anthropology Statistical Laboratory, 1945).
2. Clara A. Ridder, *Basic Design Measurements for Sitting* (Agricultural Experiment Station, Bulletin 616 [Fayetteville, Ark.: Univ. of Arkansas, 1959]).

MR. LUCAS: I have one example that applies to a dormitory, but I think it would apply to a library as well. We all know that in a dormitory or in an apartment building, if a person lives near the elevator, or at the top of the stairway, or by the mailbox, he has more friends than the person who lives at the end of the hall. This fact has been generally accepted among sociologists. It is not true because the person is particularly lovable; it is just that he is processing more people, he sees more people at the top of the stairway, or by the elevator, or by the mailbox. This would mean that in planning an office, let us say—and I hope I can relate this point to the library—if there is a director of public relations, or an office manager, or someone whose job is to be literally out in front of things, his office should not be placed at the end of the hall, but instead in the main stream of movement.

Applying this principle to a library, I would say that consideration should be given to areas where persons from different disciplines or departments could meet and actually talk—not in loud tones but perhaps in a hoarse whisper—and at least compare notes. Encouragement would thus be afforded this kind of intellectual cross-pollination between disciplines, as well as between the expert and the average John Q. Citizen who comes into the library to study or to read. This may not be a very exact answer, but I am sure that what we have learned in other fields, in sociology and especially in social psychology, can be applied to many aspects of the library.

Question: Could the panel members give us an idea of what percentage of floor space should be allocated to informal furnishings in a library?

MR. VAN BUREN: There is a general formula that, as I recall, specifies about 80-20 in public libraries and about 90-10 in academic libraries. This is not an absolute figure but a rule-of-thumb guide.

Question: What is the rationale for this amount of informal furniture? Why 10 percent; why not 30 or 50 percent?

MR. VAN BUREN: When I said that the 90-10 formula was a rule of thumb, I meant just that. This is the way it happens to work out in most buildings. There is no actual mathematical formula or proof behind such figures. The ratio can vary greatly from library to library. For example, in public libraries it can vary with the type of population served.

MR. NETSCH: I would say that it is impossible to arrive at any formal percentage. Such percentages must be considered averages. As already stated, the use of the particular space is the determinant; the kind and quality of library determine the amount of space devoted to the informal functions of a library. As I tried to in-

dicate, the use of the individual environment is increasing, and the attitude of librarians and library consultants toward this demand for informal seating is changing, so that we are likely to see much more of it in the future.

MR. CAFIERO: One of the problems designers have to face is this attempt to reduce everything to a formula. It simply does not work. In the last analysis, the problems of a particular building or a particular library determine what percentage of floor space will eventually be used for a given purpose. This may be a flexible percentage or it may be planned so that it changes as the use of the library changes. We should not tie ourselves down to formulas as we explore particular problems.

Question: I would like to ask Mr. Van Buren if he is including, in the figures he just gave, carrels as part of the total furnishings?

MR. VAN BUREN: I knew I was sticking my neck out by citing any formula because, as was pointed out a minute ago, formulas are dangerous things. The formulas I referred to, which are very loose ones, were for all public seating including carrels. It should be stressed that too often librarians enter upon a building program and say so much a square foot for this, so much for that, and so much for building costs. These are dangerous assumptions. I have seen library buildings built for as little as $12 or $14 a square foot. I read once of one built for $55 a square foot. So when you ask for formulas, this is a dangerous question to answer.

Question: My question is directed to Mr. Risom, who recommended that we use more wood in our libraries. I understand that walnut is becoming increasingly scarce and hence expensive. How does this affect your design in wood, and how will it affect librarians who must buy that wood in years to come?

MR. RISOM: First of all, wood furniture does not mean only walnut. We happen to work frequently with walnut, and I am very familiar with the problem we are facing right now. However, I am not greatly concerned about the shortage of walnut. Ten or fifteen years ago we were all worried that we might run out of it some day. One of our problems is that we are exporting well over 50 percent of our American walnut—an unusually large amount. I think the situation is going to change in the future.

One proposal, now under discussion, is to use thinner veneers in order to get a better yield from the trees. Undoubtedly an effort will be made to cut slightly thinner veneers, but these veneers present a great many problems for the manufacturers who make the furniture. I do not think we need be concerned at the present with a shortage or about the cost of walnut, which probably will not change much for some years to come.

When I spoke of the use of wood, I was not thinking of walnut alone but of all woods. Oak or any one of a number of other hardwoods are desirable. I am more concerned with the use of wood generally. Its texture, warmth, and other natural characteristics have, I think, a pleasant effect on all of us.

As furniture manufacturers, we have to develop better ways of seasoning and finishing our wood so that maintenance problems are decreased. I do not believe that maintenance problems disappear with the use of metal furniture. Wood is still a practical material to work with, and one that can be handled easily on the job. As far as maintenance is concerned, we can use oil or synthetic finishes. I am stressing the characteristics—shall we say, the romance—of wood, the patterns of the grain, the texture of it.

Question: I am an architect, and I question the wisdom of putting so much emphasis on comfort, contours, posture, and the like. When we go into a library, are we supposed to be as relaxed as possible? If there is no limit on what kind of posture people want, just think what it will mean. In order to have only lounge chairs, which require much more square footage per reader, more space will be taken up. Are we putting our money in the right place by placing so much emphasis on comfort, and contour, and posture?

MR. NETSCH: First of all, I think we have to go back to the subject of the day, which is informal furnishings for the library. No one has suggested that all libraries are going to be 100 percent filled with informal furnishings. We were trying, each of us in a different way, to define where and how such furnishings could best be used. I was attempting to show, in my photographs, the extraordinary adaptability that human beings have, which to me is not a negative response to our society. I do not want us to change into apes with banana-peel orientations. Also, I do not think that we ought to be concerned because one session out of the total program is specifically devoted to areas of informality and thus involves, automatically, some consideration of a higher degree of comfort.

MR. LUCAS: Sometime ago, Northcote Parkinson wrote an article, "How To Tell When You Are Obsolete."[1] In his typical way he seemed to overdraw the point. It was his thesis that when a company or corporation has a brand-new international or national headquarters, all furnished with excellent taste, and everything is running smoothly, the company is going downhill. The firms on the way up are those that work in Quonset huts with boards thrown over puddles of water, where the staff is so busy running around doing things that it does not have time to stop and think about its corporate image. This thesis is certainly overdone, but Parkinson probably has a point. As far as libraries are concerned, I would like to say that in this whole consideration of informal furnishings, we are concerned with needs that are fairly well down the scale of importance in terms of money spent in the library.

We would probably all agree that the single, most important category of expenditures in a library should be for books. The book collection of the library and the way the library is administered are far more important than the informal furniture. The problem is, how can we assist you, how can architects design interiors and furniture designers create furnishings to help you stimulate this feeling of adventure, excitement, and experimentation in the library? This is the provocative aspect of the problem. It really does not matter whether the reader sits on orange crates or not. The important things are the book that the man is reading, and the man who is reading it. We know that he could read it eight feet under water if he wanted to learn badly enough. I begin to sense overtones here—if we had the right furnishings, we would have a smarter public. I do not think this is the case, but I *do* think much more can be done to draw people into libraries, to make them glad to be there, and perhaps to stimulate them into reading.

MR. VAN BUREN: I do not quite agree with the orange-crate bit because I tried one once. But I think we should ask ourselves exactly what we mean when we say "comfort." Comfort for what? For what sort of activity? People are too apt to think of comfort as a featherbed or something to sleep in; but a certain type of comfort may be a bench that somebody is intending to sit on for five minutes. This is still comfort of a sort. The word "comfort" is a relative thing.

MR. CAFIERO: I got the same impression from listening to the panel. Perhaps we have tended to overemphasize the idea of comfort, but what we are trying to do is to make a point. The plywood chairs discussed earlier are essentially comfortable chairs, although they are by no means overupholstered and certainly they are not plush in the quality of materials they use. They are hard-surfaced chairs, but they happen to be extremely comfortable. We are striving not to make the furnishings in the library plush, but to ensure that the items we put into the space

1. Northcote Parkinson, "How To Tell When You Are Obsolete," *Harper's Magazine,* 215: 36-39 (Sept. 1957).

are well made, well designed, and comfortable, whether they be benches or heavily upholstered, high-backed chairs. This is the idea we are trying to get across.

MR. RISOM: Obviously this subject is an important one. We did not intend to overdo it. What we are talking about is seating for library use. We want users to spend time reading good books, rather than to get up because the chairs are too uncomfortable. We are talking about body support, whether the person is seated at a table writing or comfortably in a low chair while making notes. This is the problem that furniture designers and manufacturers are confronted with—to create the type of seating that supports the body so that medical bills do not follow afterward just because a young person or an adult likes to go to the library. We are not talking about luxury or excessive comfort. Body support has nothing to do with the thickness of the upholstery or the softness.

Question: I want to ask the manufacturers what materials they recommend for coverings for informal furniture: cotton, leather, or what have you? Second, if you use fabric in a library, should you stain- and waterproof it before you use it?

MR. CAFIERO: This is a very good question. A number of ideas recently have tended to set false standards. Fortunately, some of the synthetic woven fabrics now available are unusually strong and have long-wearing qualities, so much so that we have had to reanalyze our standards of fabric design because of them. The obvious recommendation is to use any of the plastic upholstery materials or even leather. They are the best answer to maintenance-free upholstery. At the same time, some of the plastic upholstery fabrics have characteristics that make them quite uncomfortable to sit on for any length of time. A number of the new synthetic fabrics—nylon or combinations of nylon and wool—are good, sturdy fabrics. They will wear very well, indeed.

As for stain- and water-resistant treatments, I think they help to a certain degree, but they are definitely not going to keep fabrics spotless indefinitely. With time, these protective coatings lose their effectiveness. They do help resist soil and stain, however, and I would recommend their use. We have found, in many commercial installations, where there is very heavy use—especially on the arms of chairs—that a well-organized maintenance program is an essential to keep fabrics fresh and good-looking over a long period of time.

MR. RISOM: May I inject a little philosophy on this? Here, again, I do not think there is any formula to be followed. Today, we have more synthetic materials that will last longer and stay clean longer than we have ever had before. In each case, you have to test carefully and look at what you are getting and the type of use to which the material will be subjected.

We sometimes try to overdo this business about indestructibility. Of course we should keep in mind, especially as far as children are concerned, that libraries are educational institutions. I see no harm in teaching them to take care of the equipment in the library. Nor should we look only for indestructible materials. For example, I do not think we should consider metal because somebody might carve his name in wood arms, or plastic laminated tops because wood requires refinishing or touching-up. We should look for better finishes, but I feel strongly that we may have gone too far in looking for materials on which cigarettes can be thrown, or a flaming sword, and all that kind of nonsense. There are some things we are not supposed to do to furniture.

We have better materials and better manufacturers, and we can do a better job than ever before. But let's not overdo it by giving up the texture and looks of fine furniture. We are now getting excellent woven materials in nylon, quite different in appearance from the regular, flat vinyl surfaces and only a little less practical. A certain amount of maintenance money must be spent. It just cannot be avoided. We have done considerable work over the years for the Y.M.C.A., which probably has a much more serious problem with destruction than most libraries. Over the years the organization has adopted a very intelligent program of providing its lounges, some in very tough neighborhoods, with better furniture, including more woven fabrics and better woods. The directors know they are going to have some replacement problems, but they are willing and able to police the lounges and to pay for proper maintenance in order to make use of more attractive materials. The proof of the program is that the young people still come in and are far more careful with the furniture, being anxious not to spoil anything. With the vinyls and other indestructible materials, they did their best to try to damage them.

Question: We are furnishing a small branch right now, and in my homework I came across the statement that polyester finishes may be even better in some situations than the plastic laminates. I would like some comment on this from our experts.

MR. RISOM: There has been considerable discussion of the polyester finishes, or shall we say scratch-resistant finishes, that can be applied to furniture after it is made. If the polyester finish is well applied, it is excellent, and you should definitely consider it. Have it tested and discuss it with the manufacturer. Whether it is better than the plastic laminate finish I do not know, but it is far more attractive because it can be applied on top of natural wood veneers, whereas the plastic laminate is a photographic surface which is, at best, an imitation. I am allergic to that. I think you will find the polyester finishes most satisfactory if you work with the manufacturers and designers in specifying the type to be used.

Question: What furnishings, if any, should there be for smoking? It seems to me that smoking would fit in with informal furnishings, because I get the impression that smokers feel it is a comfort. Never having smoked in my life, I do not know. Should there *be* smoking in a library in the first place? If so, should it be in the informal areas only? I know that students have said to me that they felt it was most unfortunate that smoking was not allowed in the library, because it relaxed them while they were studying and they lost time by running out to take a smoke and come back in.

Perhaps this is a matter of total design because even in this present air-conditioned room some people's eyes may be smarting a bit from smoke. I understand that filtering devices are available but that they are expensive. Is it possible to furnish a library in such a way that smoking can be allowed throughout, or should it be relegated to certain spaces?

MR. NETSCH: As a smoker, I would like to be able to smoke anywhere in the library. I recognize, as an architect, that this is impossible because it does one of two things: it intrudes on the neighbor who is a nonsmoker and it overly complicates the mechanical system. In a large office building which is adequately air-conditioned and has a lower density of users than in a library, a maintenance program of cleaning the ceiling at least twice a year must be adopted since nicotine has a habit of developing stains on the return-air grilles.

The problem of determining where smoking will be permitted must be solved in accordance with a particular building and situation. In an existing library, smoking rules have probably already been established. In a new library, it will be necessary to work out with the librarian and the building committee the smoking pattern to be established in the building. The idea of restricted smoking to the outer lobby, only, presents some difficulties. However, smoking rooms, seminar rooms, group studies, and carrels that can be served by a separate unit of the mechanical system can often be utilized for smoking.

Question: About twenty-five years ago we designed a library for a large university. Considerable money was spent on it, and the building was nicely furnished and finished. When the building was opened, the president took some of his trustees and others on a tour, in the course of which they saw a student sitting with his feet on the table. The president went right up to him, pulled him up by his collar, and said, "I spent many years raising the money to make this building possible, and I don't want your feet on the table." Apparently the word went around, and for fifteen years such an incident never happened again and the building remained in good condition. My question is: is it worthwhile to try to develop furniture to encourage people to read in different postures, for example, while lying down?

MR. NETSCH: I doubt whether anyone here has been espousing reading in a horizontal position, although it would be unfair to say that we do not recognize postures for reading other than the elaborate formal position. I appreciate your particular university president's effort to keep shoes off the desk, but we were trying to propose, earlier, types of furniture which would permit a variety of postures—not to the extreme you are talking about, but to an extent that would encourage students to adopt comfortable postures in areas designed for such activity.

Question: Mr. Cafiero said earlier that, with proper maintenance, informal furniture could last a long time. What is meant by "proper maintenance"? What sort of maintenance is required to make furniture last a long time?

MR. CAFIERO: The only way I can answer that is to draw upon certain practices we have developed in commercial installations where the business of maintenance is very important. The expenditure of millions of dollars in building and furnishings is a tangible, solid investment. In the maintenance program, keeping furniture clean is a very important matter. To allow the build-up of soilage and dirt to reach the stage that they cannot be removed when the furniture is cleaned is serious, because it contributes to the rapid deterioration of finish or fabric.

We have found that in our cleaning solutions it is possible to use a little of the exact dye used originally, so that the color can be restored and kept fresh in the overall layout. Thus when the building is a few years old, it still has a sparkle and not a dreary, faded-out appearance. This practice has some interesting possibilities in the maintenance of furniture.

We have found wood surface to be one of the best materials for working, for usability, and for ease of maintenance. In supplying one of the larger restaurants in New York City, the table tops furnished were of a simple oil finish that could be kept up by the use of a little oil rubbed on at intervals. Marks like cigarette burns and the like could be scraped right out.

If you have informal furnishings, you must have some sort of a program to keep them up. You cannot let them deteriorate to the point where you end up either replacing the top or replacing the upholstery completely. Such a program is a logical approach to a building. I think all too often we get so involved in building a structure that when it is all finished we figure, well, that is the end. In reality, it is only the beginning. The maintenance of the building is part of the everyday workability of that building. It has to be planned for and worked out very carefully.

MR. NETSCH: As an architect with a large practice involving commercial and university structures, I take some exception to these last remarks. The cost per square foot for maintenance of a college or university building comes nowhere near the cost per square foot for the maintenance of a commercial establishment operating for profit. We have a maintenance procedure in commercial office buildings for taking care of the kind of work we are discussing. Where we are not involved in a profit situation, where the rental is not $7 a square foot, we have to recognize, in our aim to achieve quality of finish and texture, that the maintenance standards of the average college, university, or public library fall far below those of a commercial office building.

If we could revise our tax laws and educate our boards of trustees regarding that particular aspect of the budget, perhaps at the cost of salaries or the book budget, then we could use very elegant furnishings. We have to be realistic and try to select materials and techniques that are a response to a particular need and a particular problem.

Question: I would like to ask the members of the panel a question about the trend in informal furniture. Do they find in their work that they are called upon to use more informal furniture than previously? With respect to informal furnishings, do they have any idea of the segment of the market that they control? As we know, the members represent three of the best-known furniture designers in the field, but there are many competitors whose standards are not so high. Are these competitors making inroads on the market? And if I am not going too far, I would also like to ask a question relating to something Mr. Netsch said about not having to provide so much informal seating if there is a high percentage of individual seating. Do you find that more and more individual seating is called for in libraries?

MR. NETSCH: We are discovering that more and more libraries are attempting to seat more and more people individually. Somewhat in contrast, they are also attempting to develop group work centers, either seminar rooms or group study centers. This is true primarily in colleges and universities; and as this trend increases, the demand for informal seating is decreasing. Informal seating is more related to activities such as periodical use or to certain aspects of an undergraduate library in which browsing is encouraged, and the idea of having a little oasis to flee to within the stack or within the group study areas is less important. Actually we have been doing some work on projects in which I would say informal furnishings are at a minimum.

Lighting the Library–Standards for Illumination

H. RICHARD BLACKWELL
Director
Institute for Research in Vision
Ohio State University
Columbus, Ohio

Few human environments are designed to make such concentrated use of the sense of sight as our modern libraries. Since lighting is intended to aid the sense of sight, we might well expect libraries to be among our best-lighted buildings. There is at least some evidence that this is not the case. Thus it is a happy challenge for me to be asked to present recommended standards of illumination for libraries to you. If libraries are not well lighted, no doubt it is because those of us who have devoted some years to the study of lighting needs for seeing have not made the results of our findings available in a sufficiently concise form. Let me attempt to summarize here the results of research studies conducted in my laboratories since 1950, first at the University of Michigan and more recently at Ohio State University.

Science devotes itself to phenomena which lend themselves to accurate study by known methods. This selective process does not necessarily ensure that the complex problems that often interest the user of scientific information the most will be studied first. Thus, in the field of the effect of light upon sight, we must admit that we have almost no knowledge about some of the most interesting aspects of the problem, simply because we do not know how to study them. We do have a considerable understanding of many effects of light upon sight, however, and I believe we know enough to specify reasonable standards for lighting a library.

BROAD ASPECTS OF THE EFFECT OF LIGHT UPON SIGHT

The physical characteristics of illumination, of interest to us, include the amount or intensity, the direction at which light rays strike an object to be seen, the color, and the plane of polarization. The pattern of luminescence or brightnesses of the entire environment is also of interest, and this depends upon the characteristics of the illumination and the reflectance characteristics of objects in the environment. Lighting is often described in terms of quantity (intensity) and quality, the latter term being used to refer to all aspects of illumination and brightness other than quantity. These words suggest that quality is an attribute that can be directly evaluated by a user of light, but that quantity is an intangible aspect of light, concerning the needs for which the designer of libraries must consult someone besides the user. Actually, of course, both quantity and quality of light must be evaluated in terms of their effect upon vision. Whereas a library user may be somewhat aware of some aspects of the effect of light upon sight, I hope to show that scientific evidence is our best guide in evaluating most aspects of light. In any case, light can be good or bad with respect to either quantity and quality or to both.

Seeing is a complex organic behavior involving a number of brain centers in addition to the eye. The eye receives light stimuli which are processed within the eye and in higher brain centers to provide information. Some of this information is used immediately to guide the behavior of the organism; in libraries, most of the information is stored as knowledge. An especially important class of information for our purposes is that which is used to program the adjustments of the eyes which aid in the collection of further information. What we see guides the adjustment of muscles in the eye; the adjustments then affect what we next see. I refer to the muscles which operate the iris (pupil) of the eye, those which alter the focus of the eyes, and those which direct the eyes toward one or another point in the space around them. The servo-loop involved in "simple" reading has almost incredible precision in programming the sequence of looking, seeing, and looking. The processing of information by the brain seems to follow a program which is itself largely dictated by the established sequence of eye movements and information assimilation.

So far as we know, the eyeball is not damaged by any kind of bad lighting, meaning either insufficient quantity or poor quality. It is easy to show that the effectiveness of information collection is reduced in bad light. There is some reason to believe that reading under bad light can lead to the development of ineffective programming of the information-collection process, which may become habitual. However, on this important point we do not have clear scientific evidence. The effectiveness with which a human learns while reading is such a complex affair that we have not found a satisfactory method for studying the effect of variations in lighting upon it.

We also know that bad lighting, which reduces the effectiveness of information collection, can lead to localized or general discomfort. Some of this discomfort apparently can be traced to lighting conditions which overstimulate some of the eye-adjustment processes, as in the case of repeated constrictions and relaxations of the iris (pupil). More of the discomfort apparently can be traced to lighting conditions that lead to a reduction in information needed to guide the eye-adjustment processes. Thus, bad lighting interferes with the sensory stimuli needed to control both eye focus and eye pointing. Poorly programmed focus and pointing adjustments produce discomfort that develops slowly, and indeed may be delayed until after the offending use of the eyes has been terminated. These effects of lighting require further study but, again, the study of discomfort due to poor programming of eye-adjustment functions has proved comparatively difficult.

We have clear and comprehensive data in two areas. First, we can relate, with considerable precision, the degree of *visibility* of visual tasks to lighting variables. Visibility is obviously important because we cannot learn what we cannot see. As important as this is, at least equally as important may be the fact that poor visibility leads to poor eye adjustments which lead to discomfort and perhaps to harmful habits of information collection. Secondly, we can describe the degree of discomfort produced immediately in a lighted environment by what is called "direct glare." Let me present recent findings in these two areas of our investigations before recommending lighting standards for libraries.

LIGHTING VARIABLES AND TASK VISIBILITY

Our investigations involved determining the degree to which more difficult visual tasks could be seen equally well when more illumination was used.[1] We required that our test subjects be correctly identified when we presented a small disc of light in a large field of uniform brightness. The disc subtended 4 minutes of arc, which made it about the overall size of a Snellen test letter legible with 20/20 vision. The subjects had to detect the presence of the disc in 1/5 second, since this is the length of time the eye normally pauses to fixate. We altered the physical contrast of the disc to vary its difficulty.

Data for 99 percent accuracy are presented in Figure 1. The curve labeled "1" represents the contrast needed by the test subjects just to detect the presence of the disc. This is "threshold" visibility. The other curves represent different degrees

1. H. Richard Blackwell, "Development and Use of a Quantitative Method for Specification of Interior Illumination Levels on the Basis of Performance Data," *Illuminating Engineering*, 54:317-53 (June, 1959).

TABLE 1
Lighting Requirements for Sample Library Tasks
Based on 1959 Standards for "Glare-free" Light

Task Description	Required Footcandles
10-point Textype print	0.9
8-point Textype print	1.1
Ink writing on white paper	1.4
12 easiest spirit-duplicated samples	2.1
Printed numerals*	8.3
No.2 pencil on white paper	63.0
No.3 pencil on white paper	76.5
5th carbon copy of typed material	133.0
12 most difficult spirit-duplicated samples	141.0

*Used by the German investigator, Bodmann.

of ease of seeing or, as we have called them, different field factors. In our basic experiments, the subjects were able to adjust their eyes fully before the disc was presented so that they had no need to search and scan. They were also especially well trained in detecting the discs. Other experiments suggested that a field factor of 15 would provide most users of light with sufficient ease of seeing under the dynamic conditions of ordinary seeing. The curve for the field factor of 15 is the "standard performance" curve which has been used to establish quantity requirements for different tasks.

The idea is simply this: Real visual tasks vary in their intrinsic difficulty due to their size, the distance at which they are viewed, their physical contrast, their color with respect to their background, and so on. We rate the difficulty of a task in terms of the physical contrast required to make the standard 4-minute disc equally difficult when viewed under the same conditions. The equation of difficulty of a real task to the standard task is made with an optical device known as the Visual Task Evaluator, shown in Figure 2. The task difficulty is designated by $\tilde{C}$, the *equivalent contrast* of the disc of equal difficulty. The required quantity of illumination, E_r, for the task is read from the standard-performance curve at the value of $\tilde{C}$ as shown in Figure 3. (The scales have been labeled in ordinary numbers, rather than in logarithms, to facilitate understanding of the process.) It is worth emphasizing that the level of ease of seeing represented by the standard-performance curve is only our best estimate of the illumination level needed. We can be much more positive, however, about the *relative amounts of light needed for different tasks*. These do not depend upon the field factor we select, but only upon the parallelism of the curves in Figure 1.

The required footcandles obtained in this manner for tasks likely to occur in libraries have been summarized in Table 1. Note that large, black print requires only about 1 footcandle, whereas the most difficult tasks require more than 100 footcandles.

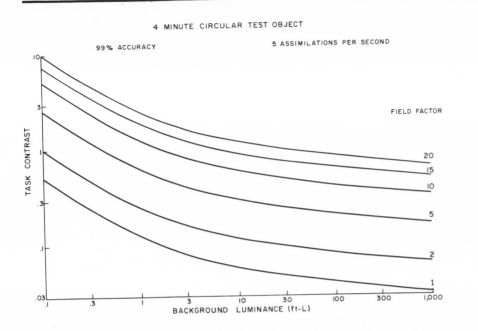

4 MINUTE CIRCULAR TEST OBJECT

99% ACCURACY   5 ASSIMILATIONS PER SECOND

FIELD FACTOR

20
15
10
5
2
1

TASK CONTRAST

BACKGROUND LUMINANCE (ft-L)

Figure 1
Lighting variables
and task visibility

Figure 2
Visual Task Evaluator

TASK REFLECTANCE OF 70%

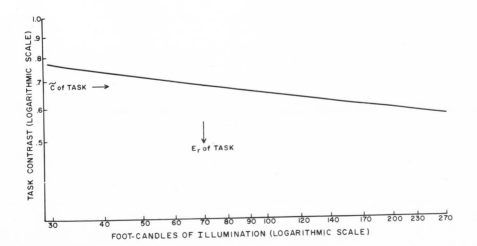

TASK CONTRAST (LOGARITHMIC SCALE)

$\tilde{C}$ of TASK ⟶

E_r of TASK

FOOT-CANDLES OF ILLUMINATION (LOGARITHMIC SCALE)

Figure 3
Quantity of illumination
versus task contrast

We must conclude that the light intensity we require depends drastically upon the task we are to perform. This conclusion supports the idea of localized lighting for areas where the *most* difficult tasks are performed. Seats near the windows in libraries have attracted those with difficult seeing tasks before this. The data certainly suggest that more light is needed for many tasks than is needed for well-printed books. Thus, if some of the more difficult tasks are performed at all generally in libraries, we have to stop thinking about general library lighting in terms of the problem of reading books alone. The Illuminating Engineering Society has recommended 70 footcandles for reading areas in libraries largely on the basis of the values for pencil writing. This recommendation makes the assumption that pencil writing is a task which must be performed throughout a library reading room—an assumption that does not seem unreasonable to me.

There has been some discussion of my selection of the level of ease of seeing represented by a field factor of 15. Use of a different field factor would influence the levels of recommended illumination considerably, as may be judged from the curves in Figure 1. It is interesting to evaluate my selection by comparing the footcandles recommended on this basis with the results of measurements of the increase of visual performance with illumination. Three published works were analyzed from this point of view,[2] with the data presented in Figures 4-6. In each case, the solid curve shows the measured improvement in visual performance as illumination was increased; the vertical line represents the light intensity recommended on the basis of my field factor of 15. It is apparent that my selection of the degree of visibility represented by this field factor results in lighting intensities well below the levels producing the highest efficiency of seeing. This represents a safety factor which is undoubtedly prudent in view of the economics of installing and maintaining lighting.

The footcandle requirements contained in Table 1 represent what have been called "glare-free" light. We all know that a strong cone of light com-

2. H. W. Bodmann, "Illumination Levels and Visual Performance," *International Lighting Review,* 13:41-47 (1962); H. C. Weston, "The Relation between Illumination and Visual Efficiency—the Effect of Brightness Contrast," *Industrial Health Research Board Report No.87* (London: H.M. Stationery Office, 1945); Miles A. Tinker, "Brightness Contrast, Illumination Intensity and Visual Efficiency," *American Journal of Optometry and Archives of the American Academy of Optometry,* 36:221-36 (May, 1959).

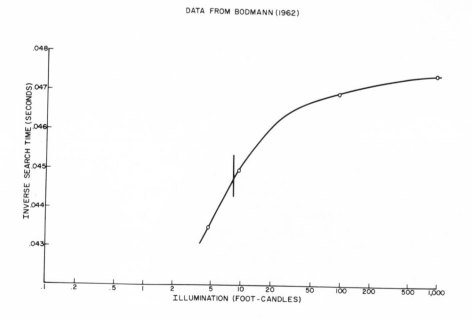

DATA FROM BODMANN (1962)

Figure 4
Improvement in visual performance
with increased light intensity

ing from the wrong direction can produce a specular reflection which will wash out task contrast and greatly reduce task visibility. Situations reducing task visibility in this way are said to produce "reflected glare." The measurements reported in Table 1 represented in effect the kind of perfectly diffuse lighting to be found with totally indirect light. We may well wonder to what extent different

methods of modern lighting affect task difficulty due to the reflected glare effect. We have done considerable work on this point in recent years.[3]

3. H. Richard Blackwell, "A General Quantitative Method for Evaluating the Visual Significance of Reflected Glare, Utilizing Visual Performance Data," *Illuminating Engineering*, 58:161-216 (April, 1963).

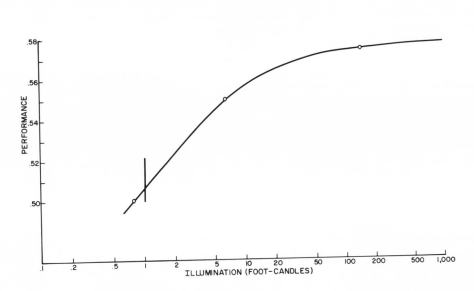

Figure 5
Improvement in visual performance with increased light intensity

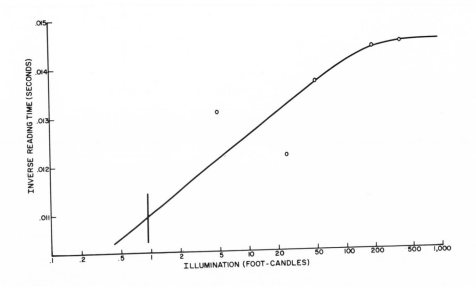

Figure 6
Improvement in reading performance with increased light intensity

Our basic technique involved making physical measurements of the contrast of a sample visual task, first under perfectly diffused lighting and then under real lighting installations. Recently, these measurements have been made with the Visual Task Photometer, shown in Figure 7. It was found that differences in physical contrast produced corresponding differences in task difficulty as measured with the Visual Task Evaluator. Hence, measures of the task contrast under a real lighting installation relative to task contrasts under diffused lighting enable us to compute measures of equivalent contrast which apply to real lighting installations.

Figure 8 shows the establishment of the required illumination—E_r' for such a real lighting installation, when $\tilde{C}'$ represents the equivalent task contrast obtained under real lighting installations. It will be noted that, in comparison with Figure 3, the value of $\tilde{C}'$ is less than $\tilde{C}$, and hence the value of E_r' is greater than E_r. This is the result generally found: Real lighting installations reduce task difficulty in comparison with perfectly diffused lighting. Paradoxical as it may sound, the only remedy is to use more of this comparatively poor light. The eye

TABLE 2
Lighting Requirements (Footcandles)
for No.2-Pencil Task
Based on 1964 Standards for Real Lighting Installations

18 by 24 foot room; 50% wall reflectance

Lighting Material	Ceiling Coverage				
	100%	78%	56%	33%	16%
Perfectly diffusing panels	82.6	110.0	113.0	191.0	253.0
Light control panels A	67.2	85.6	92.3	129.0	148.0
Light control panels B	71.1	88.9	104.0	137.0	153.0
Multilayer polarizing panels	57.9	71.2	72.5	104.0	123.0

can be helped to see either by increasing task contrast or by increasing illumination. A little more contrast is as effective as much more illumination since the increase in illumination improves vision only in what must be agreed are a series of indirect ways. *This means that illumination quality, as measured by the task contrast a lighting system provides, is much more important than illumination quantity.*

The importance of illumination quality may be judged by the data summarized in Table 2. The re-

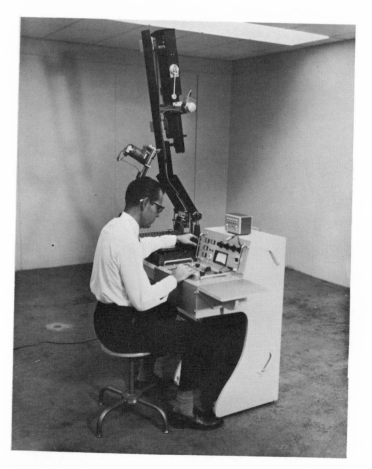

Figure 7
Visual Task Photometer

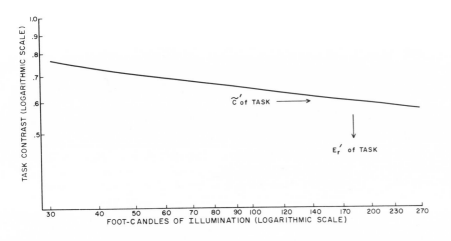

TASK REFLECTANCE OF 70%

Figure 8
Required illumination
versus task contrast
in real lighting situation

quired footcandles are for the No.2-pencil task for which the glare-free illumination requirement was originally given as 63.0 footcandles. The values reveal that the requirement for illumination quantity depends upon both the layout of ceiling-mounted light sources and the lighting material used in each layout. For best task contrast, and hence best visibility, light should come to the task from as large a percentage of the ceiling as possible. Increasing the area of the source of light reduces the deleterious effect of a light ray coming from just the wrong angle, which tends to conceal the task beneath a veil of reflected glare. The light-control materials are better than perfect diffusers in the same layouts because their control of the angle of emergence of light can be useful in reducing reflected glare. The multilayer polarizers have the light-control feature and, in addition, produce a preponderance of vertically plane-polarized light. It is a physical fact that vertically plane-polarized light reduces reflected glare, thus increasing the task contrast and visibility.

The data in Table 2 show that, with the best quality light, considerably lower footcandles can be used than with other methods of illumination. The greater *visual effectiveness* of lighting installations producing good visibility through higher task contrast certainly looms large in terms of the economics of installing and maintaining the light levels required with the various installations.

The absolute values in Table 2 depend, of course, upon the original value of 63.0 footcandles for the pencil task under glare-free light, which depends in turn upon the field factor of 15. Thus, these absolute values are subject to some degree of argument.

The relative values, however, depend but little upon anything except the physical facts about task contrast under different real lighting installations. Thus we can say categorically that the best lighting installation can provide the visibility criterion with less than one fourth of the light level required with the worst lighting installation.

LIGHTING VARIABLES AND DIRECT COMFORT

In addition to preventing indirect discomfort, which results from trying to see in bad light, we must provide light in such a way as to prevent direct discomfort. The experience of direct discomfort has occurred to us all when we have entered a room with excessively bright light sources. These sources are said to produce discomfort due to direct glare (as distinguished from reflected glare).

It is possible to set a reasonable limit on the brightness a ceiling-mounted light source may reach before producing glare discomfort. The allowable brightness depends upon the point on the ceiling being considered with respect to the location of the user's eyes. Points on the ceiling across the room are much more glaring than points more nearly directly overhead, presumably because the former are nearer the line of sight used when a person looks casually about a room. Thus, points on the ceiling across the room cannot be so bright as points more nearly overhead. This characteristic of a lighting system may be described in terms of the brightness allowable from each element of ceiling at different angles from vertically beneath it. The stippled area in Figure 9 is bounded on the bottom by a line which represents the highest brightness allowable without glare discomfort. The brightness at large angles from vertical (normal) is the brightness which will be seen from points on the ceiling across the room. Accordingly, the allowable brightness is only about 165 foot-lamberts. The brightness at smaller angles can be much higher without discomfort.

This fact about discomfort glare enables us to evaluate lighting equipment in a very general way. We must have physical data on the relative brightness of a piece of lighting equipment at different angles from vertical (normal). Then, we can consider that we are allowed to increase the actual brightness of the equipment until the brightness at some angle just reaches the allowable limit. The dashed curve in Figure 9 represents the brightness characteristic curve for a multilayer polarizer. The arrows are meant to suggest that the brightness of this material was raised until the brightness at some angle hit the lower-limit line of the region of glare discomfort. In the case illustrated in Figure 9, the allowable brightness was limited by the brightness measured 60 degrees from normal.

TABLE 3
Allowable Footcandles
without Direct Glare Discomfort

18 by 24 foot room

Lighting Material	Ceiling Coverage				
	100%	78%	56%	33%	16%
Perfectly diffusing panels	146.0	114.0	81.5	48.9	24.5
Light control panels A	421.0	328.0	235.0	141.0	70.5
Light control panels B	229.0	179.0	128.0	76.8	38.4
Multilayer polarizing panels	452.0	352.0	252.0	151.0	75.7

Once the allowable brightness for a sample light source has been determined in this way, it is a simple manner to compute the illumination produced by a lighting installation limited in this way. This value of illumination may be considered the allowable illumination without glare discomfort. Values of this quantity are shown in Table 3. We see that the light-control materials allow us to have more footcandles without discomfort than perfect diffusers do. This is because the light-control materials reduce brightness at the large angles from normal at which the eye cannot tolerate high brightness. It is of interest to note that the multilayer polarizers have the same effect to an even greater extent.

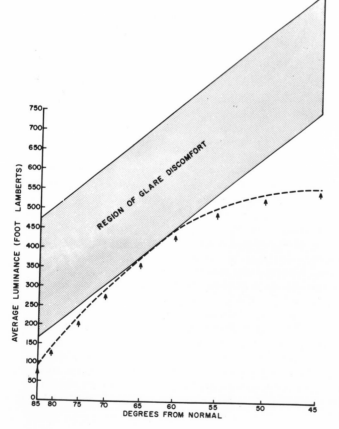

Figure 9
Glare discomfort as affected by angle of sight of user's eyes

Higher illumination levels are allowable when more of the ceiling is covered with light sources, simply because of the larger area of light source involved. Spreading out the light source obviously increases the allowable illumination by reducing the brightness at any point on the ceiling needed to produce a given number of footcandles.

It should be emphasized, as before, that the absolute values given in Table 3 are less dependable than the relative values. There is reason to believe that all the numbers in the table are too low for most modern installations. Disregarding the absolute values, however, we can say positively that the best material (the multilayer polarizing panels) permits use of more than three times as many footcandles without discomfort as the worst material (perfectly diffusing panels).

RECOMMENDED LIGHTING STANDARDS FOR LIBRARIES

Throughout the earlier sections of this paper, the theme has recurred that we can be much more positive about *relative* lighting requirements under different conditions than about *absolute* requirements. We are certain that different tasks require very different lighting levels, less certain exactly how many footcandles we must have. We are certain that lighting systems providing good task contrast can provide adequate visibility with much less light than is needed with systems providing poor contrast. We are certain that the allowable footcandles are much higher with the best than with the worst lighting materials. These statements emphasize the need for a more flexible view on lighting requirements than is implied by a single footcandle standard. The data presented in the paper should provide the designer of a library with some idea of what is involved when a given lighting system is being considered. It is clear that some lighting systems are vastly superior to others producing the same number of footcandles. When designing lighting it would seem that illuminating engineering should be at least partially replaced by vision engineering.[4]

We can draw some very clear conclusions about the relative merits of different methods of providing lighting. The worst method of lighting involves use of a few rows of luminaires fitted with diffusing panels. If such a system covers only 16 percent of the ceiling with luminaires, the pencil task requires 253 footcandles. To make matters worse, the high brightness of these luminaires—particularly at large angles from the normal—limits the allowable illumination to 24.5 footcandles. Matters can be

much improved by increasing the ceiling coverage of the light sources. Total ceiling coverage can represent the case of totally indirect lighting as well as of luminaires packed closely together. In this case, we require only 82.6 footcandles for the pencil task, and we can have 146 footcandles without discomfort. The light-control panels are helpful both in reducing required footcandles and in increasing allowable footcandles, but the multilayer polarizers are better still. The required footcandles can be reduced to as little as half, and the allowable footcandles increased by three times, when these panels are used in place of diffusers. The best system, from both points of view, is a full translucent ceiling of multilayer polarizers.

The overriding importance of lighting quality leads me to recommend strongly that this aspect of different systems be given first consideration in designing library lighting. The design must have quality, and then the quantity should be increased to the limit imposed by architectural and cost factors. Provided that we begin with quality, the "more light the better sight." As footcandles increase, more and more tasks will become adequately visible. With quality, increases in light intensity will prove helpful—at least up to 500 footcandles.

These statements imply that there is a gradation of desirability which parallels the level of illumination intensity used. At the risk of oversimplification, this gradation may be described in the following way with reference to quantity requirements in quality installations: Only the simplest visual tasks can be performed adequately with less than 30 footcandles. An increase to 50 footcandles represents a considerable improvement. A further increase to 70 footcandles is most helpful. A definite further improvement can be noted at 100 footcandles. Most visual tasks can be performed adequately at 150 footcandles.

In the entire range of visual tasks, the No.2-pencil task is a common task of about median difficulty. Therefore, it does not seem at all unreasonable to use our extensive data on this task if a more quantitative approach to footcandle specifications is needed. The data in Table 2 show that the best lighting system studied, involving a complete ceiling of multilayer polarizers, requires 57.9 footcandles. Other systems with large ceiling coverage require from 67.2 to 110 footcandles.

Although color was noted as one of the physical characteristics of light, nothing further has been said about it. We know that the color of lighting has essentially no effect upon task visibility. It has a small effect upon direct discomfort, the warmer colors producing the least discomfort. Color, of course, has very important effects upon the pleasantness of a visual environment. Here, again, we know less about this aspect of light than we should because of difficulties encountered in measuring the pleasantness of lighting.

4. H. Richard Blackwell, "Vision Engineering," a continuing series of articles appearing in *Lighting*, beginning with the issue of July, 1963.

Principles of Illumination for Libraries

BROCK ARMS, A.I.A., N.S.I.D.
President, Interior Space Design Division
Perkins and Will
Chicago, Illinois

The illumination of libraries can vary substantially from one to another and still be successful. Too often, rules of thumb resulting from partial use of scientific criteria limit our thinking on the methods of successfully illuminating a library. Some of the following principles should be kept in mind.

Visual acuity increases on a logarithmic scale rising rapidly from the threshold of sight to the area of adequate light levels, but diminishing greatly if the quality of light as well as the quantity are not controlled. The increase in visual acuity which occurs between 30 and 80 footcandles is exceptionally difficult for the adjusted, unaided eye to detect or measure. This has been demonstrated by an experiment in which one group of readers was subjected to 30 footcandles, another group to 50 footcandles, and another to 70 footcandles. At the end of thirty minutes of general reading tasks, the three groups were exposed to a series of progressively higher levels of illumination. Each individual in the experiment was then asked to mark the level at which he found the light most comfortable for reading. The majority of people who had adjusted previously to 30 footcandles indicated a level near 30 footcandles. The group which had adjusted to 50 footcandles marked a level near 50 footcandles. The group which had adjusted to 70 footcandles marked a level near 70 footcandles. Comfort as a degree of eye strain is controlled more by quality than by quantity of light.

Today most research in illumination and problems of visual acuity is being sponsored by commercial organizations rather than by independent scientists. It is natural that they should be interested in selling higher levels of light: more power and more fixtures. Very seldom, therefore, is our attention directed toward those other factors of illumination which can be even more important (within the range of 25 to 100 footcandles) than the level itself. These factors, when properly organized, can make such an installation at 35 footcandles better than one at 100 footcandles in which basic principles have been ignored. In other words, by employing these principles—which tend in any event to create a more beautiful environment—one can often reduce power costs and capital investment in the fixtures.

Briefly, this area of design can be considered in terms of brightness contrast[1] within the visual field. Brightness contrast, if greater than a ratio of 1 to 10, can cause eye strain due to the instinctive attempt of the eye muscles to adjust to both levels. Excessive brightness contrast is a result of one or more of the following conditions:

1. The actual source of a bright light being visible
2. The surfaces in the visual area being smooth or reflective enough to mirror the brightness of the source
3. The degree to which the source is a point of light rather than a diffused light so that shadows cast by the light are in sharp contrast to the visual surround

In the first instance, it is possible that an unfortunate brightness contrast ratio may result if the shield for the luminaire is dark and opaque and if there are light surfaces immediately adjacent to the light which reflect the source. This can be avoided by having the source of light high enough above the angle of vision so that it is not within the visual field, as in the case of recessed ceiling lights. However, recessed fluorescent fixtures in the ceiling of a room of broad dimensions, where the ceiling is relatively low and the lens of the fixture is visible, will introduce an area of brightness into the field of vision that can be a detriment to good seeing conditions.

In the second instance, there are several surfaces that can be a source of irritation. Glossy surfaces on desks and table tops will create conditions of specular reflection which dazzle the eye and cause it to perform its seeing job with difficulty. Many types of paper produce the same effect, especially clay-glazed papers such as those used in many magazines. The angle at which a publication is held will often minimize such reflection, but if lighting is appropriately organized this becomes less important. However, any stand or prop that tilts a book toward the reader, tends to minimize the possibility of specular reflection from the page itself. The laws of optics imply that the angles of reflection must be checked. Good seeing conditions can be achieved in some cases, not by what is done with the lighting, but by what is done with the furniture and accessories.

Some materials and colors absorb light, reflecting so little of it that if they are adjacent to materials which reflect the majority of the light a disturbing brightness contrast will result. For study conditions where reading tasks require a long attention span, it is desirable to use only materials and colors within the field of vision which reflect

1. Brightness contrast ratio is the ratio between the photometric brightness of any two relatively large areas within the visual field.

percentages of light within the allowable brightness contrast ratio of 1 to 10. This does not mean that all colors and tones in a library should be bland. It does mean that within an area used for intense study or concentration they should not produce great contrast.

Under Point 3, it should be noted that both well-diffused lighting and point source lighting can be successfully used. In the living-room environment, the reader may sit near a table lamp which, while employing an incandescent bulb that is essentially a point source of light, by its nearness to the seeing task provides good general illumination for the task area. Therefore, while strong shadows should be avoided, shadows which define the form of the architecture and its interiors are an environmental asset as long as they are not great in contrast and are not visible within the task area.

For example, bookshelves and titles of books should be well lighted, but the luminaires may be on the stacks themselves rather than in the ceiling. A reference area with movable chairs and tables should have general illumination so that if the chairs and tables are moved, the light remains substantially the same. A lounge or periodicals reading area can have lighting that is as informal as the lighting in your home—and should have such informality if it is to have the relaxed atmosphere which librarians encourage for casual reading. All of these variations are appropriate to the function, yet each is based upon the principles I have stressed. Stacks, workrooms, conference areas, general reading areas, and lounge areas are different in purpose and may evoke a different psychological feeling in us, but each, to be successful, must avoid brightness contrast and glare in the task area.

As for the psychological response to environmental conditions, it should be observed that various luminaires produce entirely different qualities of light because each type of luminaire has a different spectroscopic range. Incandescent light is very strong in the red (warm) rays; fluorescent light is deficient in red and very strong in blue and green. "Color-corrected" fluorescent tubes shed a less-blue (cold) light because some of the blue area of the spectrum has been eliminated. However, in so doing, the efficiency of the lamp output has been reduced. Generally, human skin and the materials of the building and furnishings reflect a more flattering color and are more pleasing when they are illuminated by a broad spectrum, strong in the long waves (warm range). It has not yet been possible to produce this optimum effect with fluorescent luminaires. However, such strides have been made that by carefully selecting colors and materials under the luminaires with which the environment will be lighted, one can achieve a great degree of success even with fluorescent sources. The specific type of luminaire to be installed should, of course, be employed when pretesting the colors and materials to be used in that environment. This is true no matter what luminaire is to be used.

There is much discussion about efficiency in lighting. Many promotional appeals would have us believe that if a luminaire produces more lumens per watt, it is, therefore, more efficient. As an architect, I cannot subscribe to this definition. Efficiency results when there is a favorable human response to environmental conditions. Thus, the decision of what lighting to use in a library should be based not upon whether the source is fluorescent, incandescent, polarized, or any other type of arbitrarily high level lighting, but rather upon the comfort that can be obtained without confusing brightness contrasts or glare.

The eye is a miracle of ability, and if the lighting environment is designed within the permissive approach which encourages variety and beauty, the functions of the library will be well served. Lighting should augment the visual appeal of the environment; unless it does, it is neither functional nor efficient.

Listening Facilities in the Library

C. WALTER STONE
Director
Center for Library and Educational Media Studies
Graduate Library School
University of Pittsburgh
Pittsburgh, Pennsylvania

The place of listening facilities in libraries is assured, important, and increasing. Library listening today includes use of disc and tape recordings and radio and intrabuilding communication for purposes ranging from sheer entertainment, through cultural enrichment, to provisions for information and formal learning.

The technology related to provision of listening services in libraries is complex and highly developed. It suffers from accelerated change and excessive competition among producers of audio components and systems. Acoustical and engineering studies, however, have produced abundant quantities of information needed by architects to design various sizes and types of listening space. And technical standards of a general sort have been developed in recent years to the point where a responsible layman—given awareness of how equipment is to be used and following general criteria—can select good equipment for listening and see that it is maintained properly and used well.

Helpful to librarians engaged in planning listening facilities are publications such as that developed on *The Testing and Evaluation of Record Players for Libraries,* based on a study completed for the Library Technology Project by Consumers' Research, Inc. (the first edition of this publication was issued in 1962; a revised edition is being compiled),[1] which gives valuable, objective data regarding record-player components and their performance under test conditions. Numerous technical guides and manuals are also available from commercial sources. These, however, can often be read only with difficulty by persons lacking a background in electronics.

A further ample supply of technical information, specifications, and the like is also accessible—comprehended easily by those concerned with sound re-

cordings—regarding optimum storage conditions and special techniques for inducing long and successful playback of recorded materials. For instance, as reported at some length in the Stephens College report cited in the Bibliography at the end of this paper, while disc recordings are not affected seriously by normal fluctuations in temperature or humidity, most laymen as well as librarians have come to realize that they should not be stored near excessive heat or exposed to direct sunlight over long periods since they tend to warp whenever the temperature exceeds 120° Fahrenheit. All of a library's 33-1/3 and 78 rpm records should be stored vertically in their original containers or else be kept in suitable albums to avoid warping. In any case, they should never be piled flat, stored on an angle, or left on the supports of a changer mechanism. The 45 rpm records can be stored flat because of their raised centers and relatively light weight. Special storage of recordings is generally mandatory, and, of course, careful handling is required to keep a disc recording free of fingerprints and dust and to prevent eventual distortion or destruction of delicate grooves.

Now that we live in the era of tape, librarians have also learned that to prevent physical changes in base materials, magnetic tapes should usually be stored in air-conditioned areas. Under no circumstances should they be stored or handled near any place or machinery where a strong magnetic field can develop which might tend to distort or erase recorded information. It is also known that under low-humidity conditions of storage, the plasticizing agents in a cellulose-based tape may evaporate and leave it brittle. On the other hand, excessive humidity, when present, can effect binder materials which hold oxide particles on the coated side of a tape. This results in a tendency for the oxide to be pulled off, especially in high-speed operations.

Tapes, like discs, should be stored vertically to avoid distortion of reels and to prevent the tape from settling against one flange of a reel. Whenever audio tapes are stored for long periods, there is a tendency toward print-through, which means the slight transfer of a magnetic track between adjacent layers of tape. This print-through effect can cause layer-to-layer cross talk, which will sound like a background noise when the recording is played for listening purposes. To avoid, or at least minimize, these and related effects, it is desirable to replay tapes which have particular value every three months or so on high-fidelity equipment. Such action will serve to relieve both strains and adhesions and help keep tape in better physical condition. (Parenthetically, tapes damaged by storage under poor humidity conditions can usually be restored

1. *Evaluation of Record Players for Libraries: Series II;* a report based on a study conducted for the Library Technology Project by the United States Testing Co., Inc. (Chicago: American Library Assn., Oct. 1, 1964).

somewhat by leaving them exposed for about twenty-four hours in a proper environment.) Some say tape storage temperatures should be kept between 60° and 80° Fahrenheit, and relative humidity should not range below 40 percent or above 60 percent.

In short, recording technology is well developed in the United States, and the technical information and guidance needed to select and use the technology well are widely accessible and known to librarians. Also much discussed and distributed widely through the profession's literature is information librarians need regarding selection, classification, and the circulation of recorded materials. Finding useful reviews of recordings is not much of a problem any longer, and selection procedures in libraries having major collections of sound-recorded materials appear, after normal "shakedown" periods, to develop in very practical terms. (Several items noted in the Bibliography at the end of this paper may hold some interest in this regard.)

The key problem to be encountered in planning library listening facilities does not relate to audio technology per se, or to the care, collection, maintenance, storage, and classification of recorded materials. The problem concerns administrative planning and the judgments which must be made regarding purposes and the modes of use to which a library's facilities for listening will be put.

In the public library, where use of recordings is expanding rapidly, record collections have been enlarged to include major collections of poetry and speech; recordings for language study and practice and for English speech improvement; special recordings of radio programs and historical events; as well as the ample instructional materials now being produced which range from recorded lessons on bird calls to instruction in typing, shorthand, and social studies. Public libraries which program the use of their recordings often combine playing with story telling, provide background music for special events, and introduce books and special programs of music appreciation.

Ever increasing in public library collections of recordings, as in school and college libraries, are materials developed for language instruction which, for example, in the Cincinnati Public Library now represent eleven or more different countries and are circulated with printed texts. With holdings of more than 13,000 recordings (as of 1963), which during that year were played more than 125,000 times, the Cincinnati Public Library may well have been the first of our larger public institutions to plan such special services and to include a row of built-in tables with earphones of the proper acoustical quality needed to preview or listen to records. The distinctive listening facilities and recording services provided by the Cincinnati Public Library are known around the world as vital public library services and have been publicized as such by the U. S. Information Service.

In Cincinnati, library recordings have been featured for more than twelve years in a weekly radio program of classical music. And for seventeen years "Music at Noon" was a popular library feature which, in 1963, piped an hour of recordings—"not too light, not too heavy"—to downtown listeners in the library's walled garden every day but Sunday throughout the spring, summer, and fall. Admittedly a special case, the service derived much of its being and original vitality from the first head of the Film and Recordings Center, Miss Karline Brown. Listening facilities in the Cincinnati Public Library are, then, important as well as unique, and have gone far beyond provision of commercial and noncommercial recordings to include production and replay of tape recordings of conferences, meetings, and special sessions whenever such services would have value.

But Cincinnati is not alone. The work done at the Detroit Public Library and at the New York Public Library is also known internationally. While on the subject of public libraries and listening facilities, as such, let me add as a footnote that in Louisville, Kentucky, headphones and a card catalog of recordings are both placed on a table in the reference department. A listener interested in recordings can select the poetry, drama, and so on that he wants to hear and present a call slip to the reference librarian, who then phones the audio-visual department. There the desired recording (or tape) is placed on a turntable wired to the headphone jack in the reference department, and the service loop is completed. Of course, the Louisville library is known so widely for its pioneering in audio-visual service areas that further comment is unnecessary.

In a school, college, or university, the primary emphasis must, of course, be placed on instructional and research services, with an obvious and necessary reflection of this emphasis in all library resources and facilities. But here, as in libraries serving communities, the demand for listening is increasing; the range of materials available is expanding; and individual learning through listening has become more and more a standard type of study assignment.

Now just a word concerning the special reference use of recorded materials, which also requires increasing attention. For many years, the sound recording has been the most official record kept of United Nations proceedings. That is, greater reliance is placed upon sound than upon any of the printed texts because of obvious problems of translation and the fact that so much meaning is often conveyed through intonation and inflection—meanings which a printed text cannot always convey. In a similar way, other types of historical and reference materials, collections of speeches, and recordings of special events may be important to the school or college student.

In view of the growing range of content available in forms designed for listening, the increasing variety of uses to which listening facilities may be put, and the growing demands for such services, it is my view that today no library of any kind should be planned or constructed without being wired for two-way sound. Indeed, because of the growing use of television as a monitor and carrier of all types of audio and visual communication, the two resources may well be combined.

With this statement in mind, let me identify or respond to a number of questions which, to my way of thinking, are administrative in character and which require professional answers if a library is to have suitable facilities for listening. Such questions as these come to mind first:

> What are the goals and responsibilities of the library?
> What kinds of individuals and groups compose the library's clientele?
> What are their needs and interests in books?
> And what in recorded materials as such?

With answers to questions like these in mind, the response is then easier to make to questions such as the following:

> Will recording collections and listening facilities be centralized or decentralized?
> Is listening to be an individual or a group activity?
> To what extent will tape be used: on reels or loaded into cartridges?
> To what extent will discs of various sizes and speeds be used?
> Is listening to be a one-way form of communication? Or will talkback units be involved?
> If so, what kind and to what extent?
> Are fixed and built-in facilities wanted, with related furnishings? Or are change and portability of high value?
> What special staffs should be available to organize and administer collections, supervise, or instruct in the use of playback facilities and the like?
> To what extent will a library's use of sound materials be programmed by the library itself, as distinguished from representing individual requests, selections, and choice?
> Is the purpose of listening in the library primarily a matter of preview prior to circulation of sound recordings? Or is it also intended for reference use, instruction, appreciation, or what have you?
> To what extent will the act of listening be accompanied by reading or viewing of visual media (for instance, films, slides, and film-strips)?
> To what extent will the library's interest in audio service involve production and repro-

duction as well as simple distribution of recordings?
> What about stereophonic versus monaural recordings and related equipment needs?

The list of questions could be longer. But enough have been asked to make the point. The use of listening facilities in libraries, as elsewhere, is a multipurpose activity involving multiforms of equipment and multiformats of material. Hence, the design of listening facilities in the library must reflect the multiplicity of needs and demand and should be conceived in terms of a system—economical and efficient—which relates to the services to be rendered. Without delving further into technology or architectural considerations, let us state, first, some basic requirements for the listening-service system of a hypothetical library and then draw a few conclusions regarding its optimum organization and administration within the library as a unit. Here are functions to be performed:

> Answer individual requests to hear all or any part of any physical kind of recording maintained in the library's collections
> Permit the listening by groups of various sizes to all, or any part, of an oral presentation
> Permit repetitive presentation of practice or of drill materials to aid the learning of individuals or mastery of group skills
> Serve as an intercommunication system
> Record and play back library events
> Permit a responsible individual having recording equipment of his own to select, preview, and borrow for use elsewhere sound recordings of various types
> Permit listening while reading or viewing other forms of communication with which the act of listening may correlate
> Permit dispatching through the system of any form of audio stimulus including telephone and broadcast communication
> Provide teaching-listening laboratory facilities for individual or group use

These are certainly some of the more common functions or uses to which a library's audio system might be put. They suggest to me a number of administrative and technical arrangements. With regard to nontechnical aspects of the system, I believe it consistent with whatever the library's program may be that selection of materials in sound should, as in the case of other types of resources, be the responsibility of those individuals most directly concerned with the subject or problem area covered. Similarly, those concerned with cataloging and classification of other materials in the library should handle sound recordings.

Where centralized technical control is not feasible, then it is my view, with regard to storage, shelving, and so on, that in modern air-conditioned libraries the solution can simply be one of convenience. Except for a large or very special collection, recordings can and should be located in close proximity to other materials covering the same general field of knowledge. This plan assumes, of course, that such materials are intended for use by individuals on playback units placed conveniently. From my point of view, there is little point in setting aside special rooms for storing and playing back recordings or in buying complicated machines, the individual use of which must be supervised by members of a library staff trained to instruct patrons in use of equipment.

From a nontechnical standpoint, also, materials which must be heard—like those which have to be read or viewed and which are intended for individual use ad lib.—should normally be selected and made available under supervision of the appropriate area, subject, or departmental librarian. Only to satisfy special circumstances or for reasons of cost, architectural necessity, or a similar factor, should recorded materials be brought together in an audiovisual or recordings center. Group use of listening facilities, like that arranged for individuals, should be supervised by a member of the library's staff who knows best the patron's content interests, needs, and requirements. Form and technology, in my judgment, should remain secondary considerations.

Where centralized technical control is both desired and feasible, the same basic principles can be observed, but a systems approach should be developed. My view on this is a simple one. Library listening facilities, whatever their size or type, should be viewed as parts of a network. Whatever the number or kinds of outlets, all should be linked to a central system. This approach suggests and, indeed, makes mandatory inclusion of a control area for production as well as for reproduction and channeling the full range of the library's audio resources to listening tables, carrels, headphone jacks, or special rooms. Such a control area or center would require, even for part-time use, the services of at least one individual trained technically to operate and maintain the various components housed and, depending upon the overall size of the unit and the amount of demand to be served, might even suggest additional technical assistants.

But given such a control area, or communications center operation, the rest of the system once installed would amount to little more than wires, cable, loudspeakers, plug-in jacks, and headphone units. It could perform any function listed above, should serve a large number of individual and group needs simultaneously, and would depend only upon an intercom or telephone system—whether channeled from a patron through a librarian or directly to the center—to present requests for use of the service.

I will not attempt to deal here with the complex copyright problems raised whenever a commercial recording is duplicated on tape, but it does appear that a centralized control system, manned by one or two trained technicians using equipment of high quality, can—with rack-mounted tape recorders and the appropriate number of playback units, a suitable AM-FM and short-wave radio, and the necessary intercom system—meet every demand quickly, conveniently, and ultimately at lower cost to the library in terms of wear, tear, space requirements, supervision, and listening facilities than would an equivalent service program involving decentralized use of disc playbacks, tape recorders, radios, and public address systems.

Looking ahead to a future (which probably is not so very distant) when two or even several technicians will not be able to meet and monitor all the audio service demand, we find that the technology is already with us which, employing telephone dialing techniques, can activate from a predetermined number of choices—and using only a fraction of the computer time already and increasingly available to school systems and higher education—materials which are "listenable" in any amount or variety.

At this point I think I can hear someone asking, "But what about me? My library is small. It was built a number of years ago. I cannot afford to do more than make minor adjustments in using space. What I want to know now is what kinds of equipment and facilities do I need to meet the relatively simple demands I am likely to face in the course of an average day in my school, my community, on my campus, or—in some cases—in my government agency or industrial unit?"

In my judgment the principles stated earlier hold. Listening service should be seen as but part of the total communications system. Wire the total library for sound, consistent with types of use requirements. Leave matters of content selection, processing, and the like to the established, appropriate units. Try not to create separate audio-visual rooms or departments. Regard the development of listening, as well as other forms of special electronic communication, as a technical service function to be managed and maintained by a suitably trained staff of technicians whose skills, like those of a telephone switchboard operator, IBM sorter, or computer programmer, are concerned with organization, channeling, and distribution. Then provide at those points in the library most convenient to patrons and staff alike that variety of audio outlets— ranging from simple headphones to satisfy preview requests to rooms treated for elaborate stereophonic sound systems—that the library's service program so demands.

To decide what components must be chosen, look to a communications systems engineer for help in making the right selections. But in thinking about equipment which will be required, make use of the many publications available which can suggest useful ideas. For instance, *Planning Schools for New Media: A Guide for Boards of Education, School Administrators, and Architects,* issued in cooperation with the U.S. Office of Education, was published in 1961 by the Division of Education, Portland State College, Portland, Oregon. *New Spaces for Learning,* produced under a grant to Rensselaer Polytechnic Institute, Troy, New York, from the Educational Facilities Laboratories, Inc., reviews the problem of designing college facilities to utilize all forms of instructional aids and media.

In the Federal Pavilion at the New York World's Fair, the U.S. Department of Commerce has laid out an exhibit of thirteen "Challenges to Greatness" which face our nation at home and abroad. Interesting is the fact that Education is one of the challenges but occupies only 196 square feet. One of the reasons that the "Challenge to Learning" is represented in better part than the square footage allowed would appear to suggest, is a forward-looking learning area designed and built by Sol Cornberg Associates of New York City. By means of a 30-inch-deep equipment column, three learning carrels are brought together for random selection of audio and video information and learning services. Also important in this regard is the new Communications Demonstration Center in the Hall of Education Pavilion.

Several further publications of interest are included in the brief list of references appended to this paper. And I am sure that whatever special questions may arise in our later panel discussion, my colleagues (all of whom are specialists) will be able to give detailed responses to questions concerning technical capacities of equipment, comparisons, cost factors, and the like.

Before moving on, let me report to those having a special interest in individual carrels, learning environments, or study stations and equipment that significant research is now in progress regarding optimum forms of such facilities. For example, there is the Student-Device Interface Project at the University of Pittsburgh. At Massachusetts Institute of Technology, the University of Illinois, the System Development Corporation at Santa Monica, California, and the International Business Machines Corporation major studies of automated learning are in progress. Westinghouse has just released the famous Talking Typewriter developed by O. K. Moore and others, which may open up a whole new field of individual learning approaches. Similarly, at Rochester Institute of Technology, Rensselaer Institute, Florida Atlantic University in Boca Raton, Stephens College, and Antioch College, work is completed or now going forward which seeks to establish and demonstrate the importance of new, automated, individualized patterns of learning. A majority of these—as at Grand Valley State College, Allendale,

Michigan—require an emphasis on learning carrels and listening facilities.

One additional point I would like to make before closing this part of our study on listening facilities in libraries relates to a problem which is more philosophical than technical and which, in my experience, is still more pervasive than we like to admit among our professional colleagues who manage libraries. The problem concerns a definition of responsibility. Although recordings as such have long been regarded as library materials, some librarians, when contemplating the type of communications system approach proposed, shy away from installing the systems really needed, proposing as an alternative that recordings services belong in some separate communications center or laboratory. At least this holds true for librarians in school systems and at many colleges.

For what it is worth, here is my personal view of the problem. A library is not a place or thing, a collection of materials or people some of whom have been trained especially in some way. Of course, these elements are present. But the library idea is something more and, in essence, implies a function —a function which calls for interrupting the flow of ideas in whatever form in terms of present or anticipated need and organizing, storing, and selectively channeling these ideas in the form required to individuals or groups of users where they are. In short, for the school, college, or community clientele, the library function is that which involves the acceptance and exercise of professional responsibility for making available the full range of recorded communication and information resources needed. To perform this service many professions, technical crafts, and skills are required.

Provision of materials which must be listened to and of facilities designed to accommodate listening involves only one phase of the job. Technical aspects of the service should be performed by technically competent personnel, whose gradings and rates of pay are made commensurate with the professional and service areas with which they can be identified most closely. Let us not have artificial status barriers raised to distinguish between engineering and professional personnel so-called.

To emphasize one last time, the library is, or should become, a communications and information center with all collections and services developed in suitable proportion to materials available and requirements established for their use—requirements which may or may not always be expressed overtly in statements of demand. Listening facilities belong in the library, not as isolated orphans but as integral parts of the library's total service program. Furthermore, it should be remembered that in most learning situations listening is done—most often at least—in tandem if not actually parallel with acts of reading, viewing, and the like. Finally, this brief note for the future. Materials now used to generate sound and known as sound recordings are currently being studied and modified in the laboratory with a view to making them "lookable" as well as listenable. Hence, whatever listening facilities are planned should be designed and installed with such changes in mind.

In closing, and in place of a summary, I would like to present what in a more formal paper would probably constitute an appendix. Recognizing that some individuals must choose between this or that tape recorder, record player, or other equipment now on the market and that listening facilities "in the round" are not their most immediate concern, I am adding a brief listing of specific points which I judge to be most important in selecting from present standard equipment:

1. *Avoid multipurpose units* like the plague. They are often cheaply made and overadapted and/or do not perform so well as they should to achieve any one purpose. Arguments often used in favor of multipurpose equipment are that such equipment saves money and that the library does not need to have three kinds of equipment when only one unit can do all three jobs. Actually, if all three purposes are to be served, a library may well wish to serve three different people at the same time, and better equipment can be obtained to serve all three by buying single-purpose components

2. *Whatever equipment is selected, be sure of its "systems compatibility."* Again and again librarians and educators have purchased equipment which is fine by itself but which cannot be used in connection with any other components. At times this problem has even been encountered in microphones to be used with given playback units set up as amplifiers

3. *Be sure that all components purchased maintain the level of quality desired.* Too often a very fine playback or amplifier unit is purchased. But then it is used with a loud speaker or speaker system which is hopelessly inferior and can in no way reproduce the quality of sound actually generated

4. *Buy a service rather than a brand.* In libraries a major problem respecting equipment—apart from its basic capacities—is the volume of its use. This implies a need for regular maintenance, repairs, and the like. Assuming the equipment purchased meets original bid specifications, I would say perhaps the most important factor one buys in the equipment is the guarantee and/or service program that comes with it

5. *In designing or remodeling library facilities, remember the need for adequate power sources.* Ideally, such power should be available from a floor or ceiling grid

6. *Avoid expensive cabinetwork and units which are essentially furniture.* Such furniture is high in cost, and in a library is likely to be marred quickly. Also, cabinet-mounted equipment is difficult to maintain. Rack-mounted equipment of high quality, when located in a control center and supervised by a trained technician, provides a better answer

7. *Keep in mind that interchangeability of parts is a wise goal,* unless different kinds of equipment must be purchased for purposes of demonstration. Select a minimum of brands and stay with those selected. Costs are often reduced in this manner because of volume purchasing, and repairs can be made more easily

8. *Do not circulate quality disc or tape recordings* unless wear and tear are not considered to be problems. Ideally, a master print should be retained whenever a tape is circulated

9. *Pay enough for equipment being purchased to ensure performance of high quality.* But do not be fooled into thinking that any equipment will last for all time. The average life of recording equipment—quite aside from questions of wear—can be figured in terms of its all-but-total obsolescence in less than five years

10. *Do not buy customized installations* unless responsible advice has been obtained. They are usually more costly, difficult to maintain, and lacking in service guarantees

11. *Do not permit installations used by the public, even of excellent equipment, in fixed, mounted positions.* The chances are far better than even that changes of location and systems arrangement will be desired within a few months, let alone years

12. *Remember that stereophonic sound systems required for certain types of audio presentation and appreciation may be very much more than actually needed to handle some speech or language recordings.* Buy the standard equipment needed to serve the actual range of usage planned. In short, do not buy a Rolls Royce to carry a load of coal

The list of suggestions given above can, of course, be extended to great length. Individuals interested in such matters are referred specifically to the following books for recommendations wellworth attention:

Bricks and Mortarboards: A Report on College Planning and Building. New York: Educational Facilities Laboratories, Inc., 1964.
Bruner, Bernice. "Public Libraries Utilize Non-Book Activities and Materials in Work with Children," *Library Trends,* 12:71-83 (July, 1963).
Duckles, Vincent. "Problems of Music Library Equipment," *Notes,* 11:213-23 (March, 1954).
New Media in Higher Education, ed. by James W.

Brown and James W. Thornton, Jr. Washington,
D.C.: Assn. for Higher Education and the
Division of Audio-Visual Instructional Service
of the National Education Assn., 1963.

*New Spaces for Learning: Designing College Facil-
ities To Utilize Instructional Aids and Media*,
prepared by Harold D. Hauf, Wayne F. Koppes,
Helen C. Green, and Morton C. Gassman. Troy,
N.Y.: School of Architecture, Rensselaer Polytechnic Institute, 1961.

Pearson, Mary D. *Recordings in the Public Library*.
Chicago: American Library Assn., 1963.

*Planning of Educational Media for a New Learning
Center: A Report by Stephens College*, ed. by
Ralph T. Leyden and Neal Balanoff. Columbia,
Mo.: Stephens College, Nov. 30, 1963.

*Planning Schools for New Media: A Guide for
Boards of Education, School Administrators, and
Architects*, prepared by Amo De Bernardis,
Victor W. Doherty, Errett Hummel, and Charles
Wm. Brubaker. Portland, Ore.: Division of
Education, Portland State College, 1961.

Public Library of Cincinnati and Hamilton County.
Annual Report, 1963. Cincinnati, Ohio: The Library, April, 1964.

*School Library: Facilities for Independent Study in
the Secondary School*, by Ralph E. Ellsworth and
Hobart D. Wagener; ed. by Ruth Weinstock. New
York: Educational Facilities Laboratories, Inc.,
1963.

Thomson, Elizabeth. "A Report from 100 Libraries
on Current Practices Regarding Records in Libraries," *Junior Libraries*, 85:12-13 (Dec. 15,
1960).

Audio Services and Facilities— A Panel Discussion

Moderator:
    FRAZER G. POOLE
    Librarian
    Chicago Undergraduate Division
    University of Illinois
    Chicago, Illinois

Panel Members:
    STEPHEN FORD
    Librarian
    Grand Valley State College
    Allendale, Michigan

    PHILIP LEWIS
    Director
    Bureau of Research, Development,
        and Special Projects
    Board of Education
    Chicago, Illinois

    WENDELL W. SIMONS
    Assistant University Librarian
    University of California
    Santa Cruz, California

STEPHEN FORD

My assignment is to tell you in detail about a specific audio equipment installation, and I would like to tell you something about the college before I tell you about the installation.

Grand Valley State College is a four-year, state-supported liberal arts school which opened to its first freshman class in October, 1963. When I talk about the college, I usually like to spend more time than I have available today to describe our institutional goals and how we are trying to achieve them. Now, let me confine myself to this brief statement: We are applying varied teaching methods and aids to meet the demand for individualized student instruction and in an attempt to increase efficiency in higher education. We are trying to do this by reinforcing and extending traditional methods of teaching. Three features of our instruction are frequently cited as unusual: the decentralized campus with instruction centered in small buildings which effectively combine students, faculty, and facilities; a new and important emphasis upon tutorial instruction; and an unusual and intensive application of audio-visual aids in an environmental study carrel.

The study carrel is an acoustically isolated unit containing a desk top, bookshelf, individual light, two coat lockers, two book and typewriter lockers, and paper and pencil drawers. Four carrels are arranged around a central core carrying wiring to the communications center, so that each carrel is an octagon, 5 feet high, with one face open for entrance and egress. The intent is that each carrel will serve two students. Students are assigned to the carrels and issued keys with reference to their class schedules so that there will be a minimum of conflict in their use of them. We may schedule three students per carrel during the next school year, since our preliminary use studies indicate this may be possible.

There are 256 carrels arranged in four blocks at the four corners of the library. Thus the library proper is in the center. There are only 40 seats at tables in this library; all other library seating is provided by the carrels.

The side walls and locker doors of the carrels are of perforated metal, backed by sound-absorbent material. A block of sound-absorbent material is also under each bookshelf. Overhead indirect lighting, in addition to individual lights, provides satisfactory illumination. Two sides of each block of carrels are glass walls. The 9-foot-high ceiling is acoustically treated, and the entire floor carpeted. Each carrel requires approximately 25 square feet of floor space, including access aisles and major traffic aisles from the stairs to the library area.

Although these carrels are designed partly to serve the traditional functions of a library carrel, they will offer important additional features. Half of the carrels are being equipped with a variety of audio and visual aids. We had expected that this equipment would be in operation for at least one quarter before I described it to you, but this, unfortunately, has not been the case. We now hope the installation will be completed for the use of our summer-quarter students. Therefore, I must describe the A-V program to you as it will be, without an evaluation of its successes and failures to date.

The audio equipment includes telephone-type dial selectors to connect into the audio programs through the control center. Loudspeakers and microphones are installed in the carrels, and from them students are able to listen to prerecorded lessons and to record and play back their own materials. Operation of the dial selector gives students remote control over sound programs stored in the system. There are 120 audio sources, 96 of them dial-activated. The first man to dial a cartridge hears it from the beginning, while subsequent dial-ins cut into the program in progress. Faculty monitoring of student exercises is possible from a special faculty program-control point. The carrel instrument panel also includes a television plug-in jack, and television monitors, checked out from the library circulation desk, will provide scheduled access to closed-circuit television lessons and afford opportunities for student selection of available video programs for private review.

Similar control panels, along with television monitors and camera jacks, are installed in all seminar rooms and laboratories. More elaborate equipment is installed in the major lecture halls, including special lighting facilities, local audio and camera control facilities, large screens, and overhead TV projectors.

The audio origination facilities include those for the preparation of short and long-play tape recordings for instruction in music, dramatics, and language arts; AM and FM radio tuners; four-speed record players; and audio tape recorders. Video origination facilities include live closed-circuit television presentations from all teaching rooms and laboratories, and films, slides, and demonstrations from the system control center. Also included are rebroadcast facilities for off-air programs received via UHF and VHF, as well as video-tape record and playback facilities.

All major control and selection equipment is located in a communications center in the basement of one of our buildings. Nearby are a mixing, viewing, and narration room and film and tape storage facilities. Equipment of the center includes tape decks, film camera chains, video and distribution amplifiers, multicircuit selectors for the dial system, monitors, slide projectors, audio and video tape recorders, and remote-control systems for camera operation. Conduits, already installed throughout the academic buildings, provide for coaxial cables to carry closed-circuit television signals to the control center and out to all display points. In addition, audio lines interconnect all sound outlets, and separate selector lines connect all display points to the center and to control positions.

The system can be easily expanded, and the intent is that the communications center now being installed will be extended to serve 3,000 students. At the 3,000 point, we expect to build another communications center with some cross reference between the two.

Perhaps it would be pertinent at this point to review the carrel from the student experience point as we now see it. A student uses the environmental carrel, first, as a home base on campus. This is of particular importance at this stage in our development since the majority of our students are commuters, and the carrel represents something of a substitute for a dormitory room. The student leaves his coat and books and goes on to class, returning to use the carrel as a study station, a library reading position, or for audio and/or visual instruction. He has a mimeographed weekly program guide from which he selects the program to which he has been or will be assigned, reviews previous lessons, or elects to enrich his experience. He dials the appropriate number and listens either through the two speakers at ear level or through a headset he borrows from the circulation desk.

If he is using the equipment as a language laboratory, he may respond to a dictated lesson, hearing his responses through his speaker or earphones. Or, if he is assigned to record his response, he dials the operator for a double-track recording deck which records the lesson and his response, and which he can play back for his own use or which his instructor can monitor from a console. About half of the dial-activated audio decks will be used for language instruction, the balance for assignments in literature, music, political science, and other disciplines. If the student wants music to study by, this will be possible by dialing for the University of Michigan's FM station. If any audio program he requires is not on his mimeographed guide, he dials the operator and requests that it be placed on a playback deck.

If the student's assignment or desire is for video exercise, he borrows a 9-inch video monitor, plugs it in, selects the proper channel, and watches *Oedipus Rex,* yesterday's botany demonstration, or even Michigan State University's ETV channel. He must do his TV watching according to a preplanned schedule as opposed to the audio choice which begins with the first dialing.

The complete installation was designed by Sol Cornberg of New York, with the assistance of a grant from the Ford Foundation's Educational Facilities Laboratory. Mr. Cornberg's plans have been modified somewhat to adjust to the money we were able to make available. The contractor was Chester Electronics of Chester, Connecticut; makers of the components are too various to recite here. The system is an outstanding one with few technical limitations. At the moment the only limitation we can foresee is the possibility of faculty indifference. However, all of our faculty were hired knowing this installation would be available, and most of them expressed enthusiasm about it. To date, their response has been chiefly in the form of irritation that it is not yet available.

We recently received an Economic Expansion grant from the State of Michigan that will permit us to study the carrels in cooperation with the American Seating Company. We are studying many facets of the A-V installation, such as use of the carrels with and without electronic equipment, and the effectiveness of the teaching philosophy with and without the equipment. Our major emphasis will be on developing a lighter and more portable environmental carrel which might be more easily and less expensively mass-produced. We are also experimenting with possible substitutes for the electronically equipped carrel, such as group viewing.

PHILIP LEWIS

The presentation made by Dr. Stone was right to the point. In fact, in the event that some of you think that he was being radical, I should like to go just a bit further in discussing what is in store for all of us in trying to provide services for information and for learning. The thesis I would take is that if we look at the language or the learning laboratory as a sort of communications center, then it becomes clear that the library needs the type of nerve center to which Dr. Stone referred, not only to supply items for listening and for viewing, but as an overall facility that will eventually give the kind of flexibility and services all would like to have.

Small libraries may question the cost as well as the feasibility of providing for such services. I believe the cost can be offset by the fact that proper planning of a communications network throughout a school building, or for a coordinated campus of buildings, can be done economically and with a relatively small initial investment and still provide for the addition of new equipment and services when they are needed. With proper planning, obsolescence can be avoided by using a system flexible enough to accommodate new developments as they appear.

Let me take just a moment to recite the varied systems I envision. Chicago Teachers College—North has installed a number of different kinds of effective communications systems. One is a conventional internal telephone system. A second is a parallel telephone system for dictation purposes. The third is a coaxial distribution system for television viewing and closed-circuit origination. The actual list is even longer and more involved.

Another system is that for data recording and retrieving with which you will all become involved at some time or another. This is the same arrangement used in banks for verifying signatures and other kinds of documents from master records. We are all aware of new developments in the physical reduction of printed information. You may have seen an exciting example of this trend in recent advertisements describing the process in which the entire Bible was reduced, word for word, on a little wafer only two inches square. If we are going to have information reduction to this degree, then we must begin to engineer systems to transmit this material electronically, reproduce it at the viewer-consumer end, and store it again in the master file when we are through with it.

One of the major problems in handling the knowledge explosion is that of classifying information for storage and retrieval. It is a simple procedure to program on a computer the titles of a group of articles or book references that refer to a single subject. But when you pull these out of storage and give them to the consumer, he still has to go through all of them to determine what material is pertinent to his immediate quest. Some government agencies and other organizations are beginning to index and classify information so that it is easier to obtain material relating only to specific needs. This is a problem we shall have to come to grips with in the very near future.

What I would like to talk about now are some of the devices currently available for reproduction and storage. I make no recommendation here as to quality or efficiency. I wish only to point out some new developments. Of special interest is a slide holder with 2 x 2 slides, the back sides of which are coated with iron oxide similar to that used for tape-recording purposes. Twenty seconds of audio can be recorded on such a slide. The slide being placed in a special projector, a pickup and recording head revolves, recording in a spiral pattern on the perimeter of the slide. When the slide is projected, both the audio and the visual are reproduced. This development allows slides to be resequenced without disturbing the audio presentation. Another interesting innovation is a tape reproducer employing a tape roughly half the width of that we currently use, that is, 1/7 of an inch in width. The machine, when fully loaded, has the capacity of playing fifteen hours without a stop. Can you imagine the possibilities of continuous programming for fifteen hours? It would be possible to schedule all of the recorded works of Beethoven in a given day, record a series of lectures, or prepare any one of a number of other lengthy programs.

A new device called the Re-Kard uses a file card, the back of which is treated with magnetic oxide for recording sound. Any kind of graphic data, either photographic or written, can be recorded on the front of the card. In use, the device reproduces the sound on the reverse side so that the student has access to both graphic and audio material.

A system known as Tel-E-Dex is now in use by Western Air Lines. The customer at the terminal refers to a list of questions posted on the device and presses a button opposite the one in which he is interested. Immediately, he hears the prerecorded answer. This can be used in a number of different activities and provides a versatile kind of service. Some new recorders are remote-controlled, and a bank of these would make it possible for requests for audio listening to be filled by the dialing of a code number from any student station or carrel.

The new Bell and Howell Language Master uses cards about 3 1/2 inches wide and 9 inches long. Applied to the lower edge of each card is a small strip of magnetic tape, by means of which a voice recording can be made. The unit was designed for students who want to learn a new vocabulary in science or other disciplines, prior to doing reading in this area. The device weighs only 7 pounds and can be used either in a booth or as a carry-home device.

One of the newer teaching machines has the capability of using programmed audio and visual materials for review, for listening to, and then for duplication in the student's own voice so that it can be compared with the master model when played back. The machine offers the option of true or false, multiple choice, and other types of questions, depending upon how it is programmed. In effect, this is a self-instruction device and can be used for individual study.

You are all familiar with the many different approaches to headphone listening. We have found that tapes can now be programmed just as books can. This possibility gives latitude to the teacher or librarian in providing self-instruction services using dual-track machines with a master track that cannot be erased and a student track that can be used for practice. The applications of recorded audio are almost unlimited. Terminals for listening facilities can be installed in the apron of a conventional library table. At any given time these supplementary facilities can be pressed into service as needed.

As I indicated earlier, the language laboratory, which really started many of these developments, has been broadened in concept. It is now called the learning laboratory, the electronic classroom, or—in a more sophisticated version—the communications center. We have found that this approach has pertinent applications in almost every area of learning, not alone for languages. For example, we are now planning a new commercial high school where dictation will be taught with the aid of a communications center. Dictation at different speeds and in different subject areas (such as medical or legal dictation) will be recorded in advance. When it is transmitted to the listening station, the student hears exactly the kind of material he requires at the proper rate.

Chicago Teachers College—North has several different sizes of learning spaces. Large areas will accommodate approximately sixty students and an intermediate size, thirty students. Along the walls there are almost three hundred individual study carrels. These carrels have lockers, shelves for books, and individual lamps so that illumination is adequate for study purposes. Recently, we let a contract for seven prototype carrels to be equipped with TV and audio connections.

It is a simple matter to install a dial system for random access to prerecorded audio or video programs. The major problems are proper selection of terminal equipment and the production of effective programs. *Bricks and Mortarboards*, published by the Educational Facilities Laboratories in New York,[1] illustrates several different carrel arrangements. Some of these are rather conventional designs that can be achieved with the use of standard furniture components.

The Howe folding carrel is a new development. By lifting the dividers, good isolation for semiprivate study can be obtained. Some administrators are not completely convinced that students need environmental isolation for all purposes. They feel that if the students have headphones equipped with pads, this may be enough. I think the answer depends on local conditions and on the kind of studying involved. The standard library carrel may or may not be effective in a given situation. Another new carrel is convertible and has spring-loaded partitions that can be pushed down or raised as needed. In the lowered position the result is a table of conventional appearance.

Four manufacturers are now offering new, lightweight, video tape recorders. As an example, one of these weighs 65 pounds, uses 1-inch tape, and records 90 minutes of both video and audio on a 10-inch reel. This recorder now costs about $12,000, but this is cheap compared to what was available just a year or a year and a half ago when a low-priced video tape recorder was priced in the neighborhood of $35,000. A good commercial video recorder costs about $60,000. Just released is a 1/4-inch-tape video tape recorder for $3,940, and Fairchild has announced a prototype using quarter-track, 1/4-inch tape to do the same job for around $600. These models are not currently available, but when they are, you will be able to set up these new lightweight recorders anywhere and record any material, then reproduce it through a conventional television receiver.

Slow-scan television, using regular telephone lines, is also available. Telephone conference calls that now bring together persons in Washington, California, and Chicago, or wherever they happen to be, can also use slow-scan television to provide the visual element. The future communications system for the library will be a coordinated service employing many equipment elements to serve the library's clientele more effectively.

WENDELL W. SIMONS

Today you have heard the terms "systems" and "systems planning." I use the term "programming" to designate what Dr. Stone and others have called systems planning. That is to say, I believe a listening system should be cohesive throughout. It should be comprehensive, not piecemeal. I am afraid in audio-visual design we tend to buy out of a catalog without knowing exactly what we want to accomplish and why. So I would like to emphasize the importance of this word "programming."

Installations as complex and expensive as those the previous speakers have discussed are important undertakings. Such systems should be programmed. In fact, they deserve a carefully conceived, written program such as you would prepare for a library building. What I plan to show you is a rather simple exercise in programming a listening facility. I have chosen to concern myself with only a record-playing situation, but the same principles can be applied to installations for large-scale tape recording, video, or any other of such media.

Figure 10 shows what we may call the four basic modes of record listening in the order of their cost

1. *Bricks and Mortarboards: A Report on College Planning and Building* (New York: Educational Facilities Laboratories, Inc., 1964).

of installation—a very arbitrary order. Notice that individual control of the equipment is separated from staff control of the equipment and that earphone listening is separated from loudspeaker listening, which requires a room or some kind of enclosure.

Figure 11 shows the first mode in detail. The rectangle at the top represents the control point from which records may be checked out. Below are listening stations where the individual has a record player to himself with a pair of earphones. This does not require any architectural enclosure and, of course, is considerably cheaper than other designs. We may assign relative cost estimates to these different systems. Actual prices are not important. This installation could cost $50 or $500, depending upon how far you wish to go into high fidelity. For the purpose of this discussion I have assigned these basic prices: turntable and arm, $75; amplifier, $75; earphones, $25—a total of $175 to equip one station under these conditions. That includes the playing source and the listening device. This would be a moderate, run-of-the-mill cost for this kind of equipment.

Now, what kind of capability does this situation have to adjust to changing work loads from day to day? Actually, not very good. On one day there may be a heavy run; on some days it may be a Beethoven symphony or some musical work, on the next a Shakespeare play, a historical record, or poetry. With equipment of this configuration, you can change to accommodate different loads only by plugging in more phones to a given player. If a person is sitting at a table with a record that fifty people want to hear on the same day, you are in trouble, because only a limited number of earphones can be plugged into one player.

This means that in order to cover such heavy use records will have to be duplicated. Many of these will receive heavy use only at given times. This is a minus factor because it requires a duplication of records. The third point is obvious. Here the public is handling the records, and the records will undergo considerable abuse and have to be replaced often. So the expense in maintaining the records is great, both in duplication and in replacement.

In Figure 12, the second of these configurations, we are still dealing with earphones, but now the record players (the program source) are on a single control table. With this configuration, consisting of three record players, the expense is slightly more per one-unit station because the cost of wiring the control table to the listening points must be added. The cost of wiring will run about $20 per station, which is not significant but is slightly more expensive.

With this situation you have the ability to shift with changing work loads from day to day or hour to hour. You can feed one program into one station or into any number that may be necessary; you can

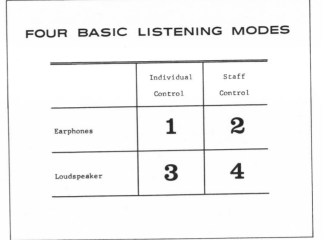

Figure 10
Four basic listening modes

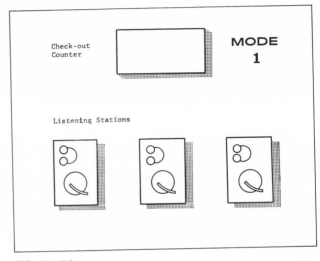

Figure 11
Listening mode 1

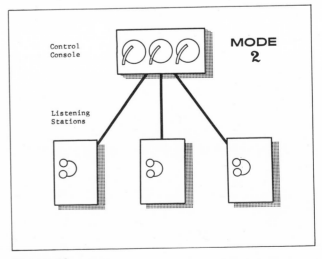

Figure 12
Listening mode 2

even feed individual, separate records to each separate listening post. This results in considerable flexibility. Essentially, this is the mode used in many study carrels, although it is a highly simplified version of systems you have been hearing about today.

With this mode, we have eliminated the need for excessive record duplication because the record can be duplicated by feeding it through many lines at one time. We have also eliminated the problem of wear and tear caused by public usage and mishandling. From this standpoint the system is a plus. It gives good economy and is relatively inexpensive to install.

The third mode (Figure 13) shows a typical listening-room situation. This is similar to the installation at Washington University: a small listening room, an individual record player, and a loudspeaker with no wiring and no connection to the control desk. Here, on the same basis as the earlier figures, the cost runs about $75 for the amplifier, $75 for the speaker, $75 for the turntable, and about $500 for the room. This is only an estimate. The installation might run much more or could be built for less, depending on how soundproof the room must be. Obviously, the room itself increases the cost considerably. The ability to adjust to a changing work load is important because each person in a room monopolizes the record. Only as many people as can crowd into the room can listen at the same time. Again, the records need to be duplicated, and the same problem of wear and tear occurs because of handling and mishandling by the public. So on economic counts, alone, this is a minus situation.

In Figure 14, we have the listening room again, this time wired to a control desk. Here the turntables have been taken out of the rooms and there are only speakers, with control of the records at the console. The cost is about $20. The wiring and the ability to adjust to changing demands are good. With a central console it is possible to feed one program to all rooms or to feed individual programs to each room as the work load may require. The need for duplication of records and the need for heavy replacement because of wear have been eliminated. Economically, this mode is a plus. Now, consider Modes 1 and 3 again, and note that they involve individual control by the listener and are rather uneconomical from the standpoint of excessive wear to the record collection. In addition, they are less easy to schedule because of their inability to adjust to shifting loads. Modes 2 and 4, involving staff control, give good flexibility and are more economical to operate in terms of maintaining the record collection.

Without being dogmatic I wonder if these modes have gained such wide acceptance simply because they are convenient for the staff and they represent an economy. They do not, probably, best serve the needs of the user. Let us review these modes again

from the standpoint of the user or listener. I have made no detailed study or tried to analyze psychologically what a listener needs or wants. Instead, these are observations made in dealing with an academic library and with college students over a period of some ten years.

First, in Mode 1, the user seeks a certain amount of comfort. If he sits for an hour or several hours with earphones on his head, even under the best circumstances he can become very uncomfortable—at least most people do. Secondly, I believe it is safe to assert that earphone playback does not yet, and probably never can, give as high a quality of reproduction as a loudspeaker system. I hasten to add, however, that earphone design has improved tremendously in the last few years, and I would not hesitate for a moment to furnish good earphones as a listening medium.

The addition of the large pad, which may look like a Martian space helmet, has made a great difference. It not only adds to the general comfort, but takes the weight off the ears and puts it on the firmness of the head; it also aids listening pleasure by keeping the music from escaping out the sides. It is the pad that makes the difference, and I would recommend that no earphones be bought in this day and age without them. Nevertheless, I think it is safe to say that earphones do not give as good a reproduction, nor are they as comfortable, as a loudspeaker. I believe, from this point of view, users would prefer a loudspeaker rather than earphones.

The matter of individual controls is significant in serious listening to recorded music or literature. Normally, a student following a score is unable to listen to a complete symphony or other musical work straight through; he wants to work at his own pace. Perhaps he wants to hear a passage over and over; perhaps skip one and move on to the next; perhaps go back to the beginning. Thus, individual controls here are of primary importance. The same thing is true of following a play. In many recorded plays, particularly long ones such as those of Shakespeare, there is a tendency to record them on a limited number of discs and thus to leave out extraneous parts of the material. In following a printed script of such a play, the student may have difficulty in following the text. If so, he wants to be able to stop a record and concentrate on a particular part. He needs to have the ability to stop, to go back, to skip, to move around. I do not believe this can be done effectively through a remote-control situation.

Perhaps the dial systems will, in time, give the user complete control and flexibility. If so, this will be wonderful. Certainly, this is the direction in which I hope such equipment will move. At the moment, I think individual controls still serve this kind of use best.

In Mode 2 (Figure 12) again we have earphones, and again the same comments apply. The earphones are not so comfortable and do not give the quality of reproduction that a loudspeaker would. Again, the lack of individual control in this situation, where sound is piped from a central place, is probably not acceptable in all instances but may be in some. There may be individuals, in fact, who prefer not to have to handle the control but would rather have it done for them. I do not ignore this possibility, but I do say there is definitely room for conjecture and opinion here.

In the next mode (Figure 13), showing the loud-speaker rooms, I believe most listeners prefer complete control over what they are doing, what they are hearing, what they are listening to. In this mode, the loudspeaker is connected to a central system, and students still have the comfort and the good fidelity of the loudspeaker but with the controls taken away. I do not believe this satisfies all listeners.

Now let me sum up. I have gone through these modes twice, once from the viewpoint of economy and what I believe is staff convenience and, second, from the viewpoint of convenience and pertinence to what the user is doing. I think we find quite a conflict here. Mode 2, the one involving earphone listening from the remote point, was the most economical and the most practical, the most efficiently operated by staff, but the least desirable from the standpoint of the listener. Mode 3, the loudspeaker rooms with individual controls, is the most desirable from the listener's standpoint, but is the least economical and least desirable from a staff or administrative standpoint. Modes 1 and 4 fall somewhere between these two extremes.

Let us consider one more aspect of the user and his approach to these situations (Figure 15). Dr. Stone touched on this with four components; I have only three. I call them "listening levels." They are: mass assignment, with which we are familiar in college or high school; individual study, which can occur in any kind of library; and recreation, which includes cultural listening, general listening, and background music. I think these three levels have different requirements from the viewpoint of the listener.

A mass assignment, as we know, cannot possibly be handled by individual students using individual machines. A hundred copies of a given record cannot be supplied for a hundred students in one music or English course. What is needed is centralized control, centralized piping of a record to many stations, whether these are individual earphone stations or a loudspeaker station in a large classroom. I suggest that these are the answer to this kind of mass problem, where, on a given day, a hundred students will be wanting to hear the same record.

The best solution is to have this program source connected to a classroom or assembly hall or to a large room not necessarily in the library, perhaps in a music building or elsewhere. Here, then, in

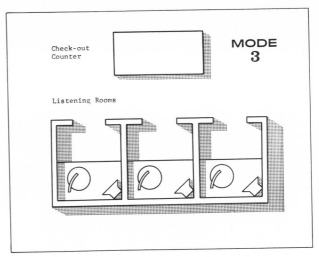

Figure 13
Listening mode 3

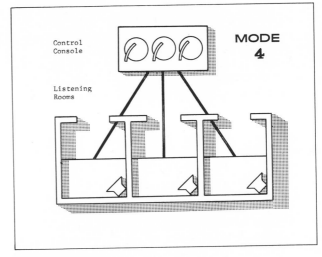

Figure 14
Listening mode 4

LISTENING LEVELS BY MODE				
	1	2	3	4
Mass Assignment		✔		✔
Individual Study	✔		✔	
Recreation	✔	✔	✔	✔

Figure 15
Listening levels by mode

Mode 4, loudspeaker listening, remotely controlled, is the best way of caring for mass assignments. Mode 2, earphone listening by remote control, is the second most effective. For individual study, the loudspeaker situation with individual controls is the best, and individual controls with earphones is second best. For recreational listening, where the needs are less specific and less demanding than in other situations, any mode will probably serve, but not at the same cost. Mode 3, however, is probably most satisfying to the greatest number of people.

Situations vary, of course, from academic libraries to public libraries. Public libraries may be able to ignore the problem of mass assignment; perhaps not. Some academic libraries may choose a certain kind of listening. This is an individual choice. My presentation was an exercise—in effect, an exercise I have done myself as a design for a new facility—and I wish to point out this rather direct conflict between efficiency for staff and convenience for user. The answer must be a compromise. I do not believe there is one system that serves every purpose fully. We need to provide several modes in order to take care of a variety of needs.

As the checks in Figure 15 indicate, I think Mode 3 is the first and most essential for most academic library listening. Mode 4 (loudspeaker listening, remotely controlled) is also important, and as a third choice I would suggest Mode 2, an earphone listening setup remotely controlled. These three modes, in combination with a central console, provide considerable flexibility and should take care of the major needs of the user. Above all, I think we need to consider, in programming, what the needs of the user are. We must use caution when we buy out of a catalog and not think only of cost and convenience from the staff point of view. More important is consideration of what a user needs and what he desires. You will recognize that I have taken the extreme middle position.

Discussion

Question: In view of the fact that Dr. Stone has recommended that all equipment for communications should be in the library, what about the college that has a language laboratory in connection with the language classrooms? Is it desirable to change that setup?

MR. STONE: I would not like to get into conflict with my colleagues in other departments of the university, or with the broadcasters, or the language laboratory managers. I think the answer that should be given to this question is as follows: First, increasingly in every college and university, on all levels, the library is going to be more and more of a communications and information center. Where there are existing facilities, however, appropriately managed and

operated, it would seem to me that the library staff should work with such facilities rather than in competition with them. A council or cooperative mechanism could well be created that might take the form of a communications and information service group. The library then would have those additional resources needed to complement the facilities of the language laboratory, but would not duplicate what is already good and efficient.

Question: I should like to ask Mr. Ford about the four-unit booths that Grand Valley State College is using. Could they serve as portable booths in a public library? I am concerned both about their openness and about their use of loudspeakers—open as they are—without disturbing the rest of the audio-visual room. In other words, I dislike headphones. In addition, sound booths are difficult to build in and then, after about three or four years, may have to be abandoned because the library expands. Is it possible to use these four-unit booths as freestanding units in the middle of the floor and not disturb others in the room?

MR. FORD: That is one of the reasons why I said I regretted that we had not had experience with these booths. We sometimes think our library is going to sound like a public laundry because the noise level with loudspeakers may be very high. Nevertheless, although the student has individual controls, the maximum volume can be controlled by the librarian. We are also hoping that the acoustical inner walls of the carrel will help take care of the noise. The carpeting and standard acoustical ceiling should help, too. Only experience will tell us this.

MR. STONE: I would like to make a comment on the learning carrel from a different point of view. Some of my colleagues, who are architects, tell me not much is yet known about what happens in the way of psychological adjustments or changes to an individual who sits in one of these booths for a long period of time. Some view of the outside is also necessary, through window spaces or their equivalent. We are going to need a great deal of experimentation as Mr. Ford has said. The only comment I would like to give is that we must make our systems flexible, so that as we get additional insights into the reactions of individuals in this type of facility, we can make necessary changes.

MR. LEWIS: In trying to isolate the rest of the library from the sound in a carrel, if you begin to deck the carrel over and acoustically treat it, then you have to begin worrying about ventilation and air conditioning. When you put all of these items together, you are going to find that the control of individual loudspeakers presents a number of problems. Mr. Cornberg, in one of his earlier designs, placed low-level loudspeakers in the left- and right-hand sides of the booth opposite the student's ears, and tried to use this acoustical barrier to keep sound from spilling out. This is going to be a very critical problem. I would say, before you decide on loudspeakers of this kind, consider all the other factors involved.

Question: I have a question for Dr. Lewis. Is the convertible library carrel that you discussed in use in any public library that you know of?

MR. LEWIS: This convertible carrel is one that is being produced by the Howe Company. If you are interested, the representative would no doubt be happy to confer with you on it. The company is field testing it at the present time. It is not in any permanent installation that I know of.

Question: I have a question for Mr. Ford. First, I would like to state an assumption on which I would like you to comment, and then I will ask a more specific question. The assumption is that the setup at Grand Valley State College to which you referred will be geared to the needs of instruction and the interest in specific materials, but that the research needs of the student body will, of course, be directed more toward the book collection. On that assumption, I would like to know something about the cost of the installation at Grand Valley and also the number of volumes currently in your book collection, or perhaps the projected size of your book collection.

MR. FORD: I do not know if I understood the first part of your question. We make intensive use of the library for freshman research in political science and in history. We are very fortunate in having a library-oriented faculty. The book collection is adjacent to the A-V installation. The easiest way for me to give you an idea of the cost is to make a comparison of the cost of carrels and other equipment. The carrels cost about $200,000. The library has spent about $400,000 for other needs. We have estimated that if we have a student body of 8,200 and we have four classes of students, we will need a 60,000-volume library. We have been quoted in *Bricks and Mortarboards* to the effect that we would restrict the size of our library. That was a misquote.

Question: I would like to ask Dr. Stone if the same caution in the use and care of tapes should apply also to microfilm?

MR. STONE: There are those in the audience who are better qualified to respond to this, but my impression is that it does apply and you should preserve some measure of temperature and humidity control. Also, because of the recent uncertainty with regard to what is happening to microfilm materials, you need to check them periodically, but I do not know the technical answer. Perhaps a colleague here does, or someone in the audience.

MR. LEWIS: We have had some recent pertinent information. In trying to acquire some microfilm storage units, we were told that humidity and temperature control were no longer considered so important as they once were. I do not think this means you should forego all your precautions. It merely points up that we are not too sure of microfilm care. Films are now made of better base stocks and by different procedures than formerly.

Question: I am interested in the location of listening facilities primarily in a public library—a recreational type of situation. Should these facilities be in a location that calls attention to these particular services, or are there other considerations concerning location?

MR. STONE: There are two answers to that, I suppose, if we take the extreme middle position to which Mr. Simons referred. First of all, one comment I did not make during my presentation had to do with the development of the film and recording center at the Cincinnati Public Library and the very interesting approach there to a specialized facility for both films and recordings. If specialized listening areas, facilities for production and for reproduction of programmed recordings from that center through the entire library including the garden areas, and like services are offered, it seems to me that the answer to the question is not entirely yes or no. It depends on the program of the library and how the recordings will be used. I would hope that the centralized audio-visual room, recording, or listening room where that is all that goes on could be avoided, and that, instead, facilities for listening could be provided according to subject or functional areas. Of course, it may be necessary to centralize the technical controls essential to provide adequate listening. This would be my general view. The answer is yes and no in this situation.

Question: Are any of the items discussed here today obtainable in models powered by transistors? What equipment can administrators struggling with rising building costs look forward to other than that powered by cords linked to a permanent outlet? I am thinking, for example, of the new electric office clock that operates with no cords and that can be moved around any place.

MR. LEWIS: I do not think anyone here can answer your question completely. Some tape recorders, as you all know, are operated by flashlight batteries. Some phonographs now are battery operated and completely portable. I assume the same would hold true for any device except for projection equipment, which requires a large wattage consumption for light output. There I believe you will continue to need local power sources. I would say the situation is encouraging in terms of most of these devices except for projectors. Some of these developments may have to be studied carefully because the cost of portable items could go so high that they will not be economical to use. On the other hand, rechargeable batteries are now being made, and you would want to consider these.

Question: I have two questions. One is directed to Mr. Ford. I would like to hear his comment on the availability of program material for the system that he is installing. The other question is directed to anyone on the panel. I would like to have an impression of a piece of equipment that two manufacturers are currently offering—a sound center on a book truck, including both a tape deck and a record player and a number of electrical outlets.

MR. FORD: We spent considerable time discussing program material. I am not sure I know the answers for developing good material any better than you do. We have had some developed by our own faculty. However, this presents a number of problems. Obviously we expect to use a wide variety of materials, as would be normal in an operation such as ours. I think this is a serious problem and, for that reason, I believe we will be using our own faculty to the limit of the time they have available.

Question: Dr. Stone mentioned that the listening area is assured in the public library. I would like to have him comment further and support this view for public librarians to take home with them.

MR. STONE: In order to have time to think of an answer to this question, I wonder if we could take the second part of the previous question first.

MR. SIMONS: I have an opinion on the portable, book-truck-type listening facility. This, in essence, is a table with a record player and earphone attached and is one of the modes I discussed, with the addition of wheels. Since this unit is portable, it needs a plug-in every place it goes. In addition, there is a very definite trend in educational usage away from portable models as equipment becomes more and more plentiful. The better equipment is firmly mounted. Portability is another kind of flexibility, and we can gain this same flexibility by wiring. You can then keep your turntable or program source in one place where it is under control. I think this makes more sense than the book-truck idea.

MR. STONE: In response to the question about the place of listening in the public library, I think our profession is coming to recognize that we are concerned with whatever recorded communication individuals or groups need to accomplish their purposes, whether recreational, informational, or educational. As more materials become available, we see an interlocking between the types of materials that a person may require. In order to use one effectively, he has to have the others available. The place of films in libraries has been established for twenty years. Certainly, the use of film in prominent libraries all over the country—Detroit, Cincinnati, New York, Topeka (if I did not name yours, I apologize)—is so well established that no one doubts this medium is a primary concern of public as well as of academic libraries. The point I would like to make is that all types of libraries must become part of the system, each serving the other.

Transporting Books and People in the Library

KEYES D. METCALF
Librarian Emeritus
Harvard University
Cambridge, Massachusetts

I am not an architect or an engineer. I speak as a librarian with some experience about what a librarian can expect in mechanical transportation in a library. I have tried to avoid technical details. While the talk is listed in the program as "Mechanical Distribution of Books in the Library," with the sanction of the chairman I have broadened the topic somewhat. I shall discuss the movement of books and people both vertically and horizontally, that is, traffic problems in general, including those involved in the provision of individual accommodations, which in recent years have become of such great importance in our academic libraries.

Fifty-nine years ago, in September, I went to work in the Oberlin College Library—a five-level building with no elevator or booklift, no pneumatic tube, ramp, endless belt conveyor, or anything of the sort—and for three full years I was *the* mechanical transportation for the building. But in spite of this, I do not recommend high school or college boys as suitable mechanical transportation in libraries, nor do I recommend pushing book trucks upstairs, or down for that matter. Libraries should be planned without unnecessary changes in floor level, such as Paul Rudolph, the dean of the Yale School of Architecture, likes to place in other types of buildings.

I was once consulted on a library in northern New England. It had been proposed that a two-level building on a hillside, with an entrance and book storage on each level, would not need an elevator because it would be possible to put books on a book truck, push them around the building outside, and bring them in again at the other level. Thus the money a lift would cost could be saved. I, rashly perhaps, suggested that while this procedure might do in Florida or southern California, in a country which often had fifteen feet of snow in the winter it was inadvisable.

So let us agree that vertical transportation by stairs based on human labor is not advisable for books, and that mechanical aids of some kind should be provided if a library has more than one floor level. The simplest mechanical aid is a dumb-waiter that operates without power, except for a little muscle used with a pulley and weights. There is a place for one of these occasionally.

The next step is a power-driven booklift. But booklifts, with or without power to make them go, are not adequate and should be avoided if possible. No lift into which books are placed and then taken out again is recommended for two good reasons. First, there is the extra handling. Let me emphasize this point from personal experience. For five years I was Chief of Stacks in the New York Public Library. Books were collected from a stack 330 feet long and 80 feet wide and transferred to booklifts to be carried up to the reading room above. They were returned the same way. The traffic varied from 3,000 volumes a day, each way, up to 7,000. That is, 6,000 to 14,000 books were literally thrown into a booklift, and the same number taken out. Boys, or girls for that matter—to say nothing of grown men and women when working on that scale and always in a hurry—tend to be careless with the books.

It would not be an exaggeration to say that on a 10,000-volume day $1,000 worth of damage was done to books and bindings. Some of it was reparable, of course, by rebinding, but costly just the same. Much of it was irreparable as a large percentage of the great collections in the library was irreplaceable. I am glad to report that these booklifts were replaced by endless belt conveyors many years ago.

Booklifts have a second disadvantage—one which did not apply in the New York Public Library because of the size of the staff there. Unless there is someone at the other end of the line to take the books off the lift, the person who puts them on must climb the stairs and take them off himself. This may be better than carrying the books upstairs by hand, but it is still hard on them.

The next step above a dumb-waiter or regular booklift is a lift large enough so that a book truck can be wheeled into it. The door must open to the floor, of course. There is no basic difference in the lift's operation, but it may save two extra handlings of the books. There is still the disadvantage of requiring someone at both ends of the line. If the lift can be made large enough for an operator with the book truck, so much the better, but it then becomes a small elevator. There are fewer booklifts in libraries today than in the past, and many of those that have been installed are seldom used if an elevator is available in the building.

Elevators can be found in most libraries, except very small ones. They present a number of problems. First, they take space: space for the car, space for the shaft, and space for a lobby for access to the elevator. Do not cut down too much on the lobby space if you expect any considerable amount of traffic; congestion will be sure to result. The square footage used is expensive and, remember, it is repeated on every floor to which the lift goes. Space is also required for the machinery, which preferably should be at the top. If the roof is flat, the space may have to be in the form of a penthouse which will show from the outside and to which many architects object. The machinery can be placed in the basement or subbasement below the regular levels, but this solution, I understand, is not so satisfactory from the engineering point of view. In addition, the excavation may be difficult if bedrock is involved, and there may be a water problem. But whatever you do, do not fail to have the elevator go up to the top levels of the building even though it requires a roof penthouse. I have known of elevators not being carried up to the top levels for architectural reasons, and as a result of this and other problems that could readily have been avoided, a $2,500,000 building only ten years old had to be given up and a new one constructed.

But to come back to the space that the elevator will require. Be sure that the cab is large enough, always keeping in mind that the cost of the elevator depends to a considerable extent on its size and the amount of weight it is to carry, as well as on the height to which it is to rise. Two elevators cost more than one, although two small elevators will not cost twice as much as one big one. The advantage to two elevators, of course, is that if one gets out of order, the other will still be available. If there is to be more than one elevator, the question arises as to whether they should be located side by side or at opposite ends of the building in order to save steps. Two elevators placed side by side will do the work of at least three that are widely separated but, of course, they will inevitably involve more walking. Decision must be reached as to which alternative is preferable. The five widely separated elevators in the Widener Library at Harvard are inadequate. Three in one bank would have been much better.

The location selected for an elevator is a matter of great importance. Elevators serve two purposes: they provide for the transportation of books and of people. Both should be kept in mind.

Only a large library can or should afford more than one service elevator. Where should it be placed? Librarians have tended to think that if the shipping entrance is on a different level from the processing staff and there is only one service elevator, it should be next to the service entrance with the acquisitions department immediately above it. This position has often proved a mistake because the amount of material that comes in to a shipping entrance in most libraries represents only a fraction of that which is handled from the circulation

desk, with books being carried back and forth from different levels for use by readers. If there is to be only one service elevator, place it as close as possible to the circulation desk and do not worry too much about transporting books from the shipping room to other parts of the building.

An elevator may be used for transportation of readers, as well as of staff and books. If there is only one, try to place it where it will be convenient for all three. Remember that if the elevator is readily available to readers, they will use it, whether they need it or not. I know of one large library with only three levels, one up and one down from the entrance. Apparently no student here would think of using the stairs. The result is that the elevators are overburdened and tend to get out of order. If you want to prevent elevator use by persons for whom they were not intended, they must be restricted in some way. This can be done by having them operate by key only. Do not hand keys out indiscriminately to all faculty members or graduate students, as they will inevitably get into other hands. If the elevator is to be available to graduate students and faculty only, place it adjacent to or within a service desk area where its use can be supervised. Even if it is available without supervision on the upper levels, there will then be little temptation to come down in it. Arrangements should, of course, be made for elevator use by handicapped persons, and a door provided wide enough to permit a wheelchair to enter.

At the Harvard Lamont Library, on the other hand, where many students go up three flights and many more go up one or two, there are no public elevators, and the students do not complain seriously about the lack of them. There are elevators in the building, but they are operated by key and available only to the staff and to handicapped persons.

The cost of an elevator will depend not only on the size, as already indicated, but also on the number of floors it is to serve; the space occupied, including the lobby area on each floor; the elaborateness of the controls; and the type of power used. Most elevators today, particularly those that serve more than a few floors, operate under electric power, but if the distance to be traveled is no more than 40 or 50 feet—or, in recent years, somewhat more than that—a hydraulic elevator or one powered by oil can be used, which will be considerably cheaper. It will also be slower, but the reduction in speed is ordinarily not serious if the distance to be traveled is not great. Oil- and water-powered elevators tend to be considerably noisier than electric ones, but the sound can be offset by a competent engineer.

Any library elevator, and particularly one used for the transportation of books, should have a leveling device. Otherwise, it will be almost impossible to stop it at exactly the right level. Pushing or pulling book trucks up and down a few inches to get them into or out of an elevator is noisy, damages the truck, and gives it more wear and tear than it would receive in months of regular use. Keep in mind the cost of elevator maintenance and repair and of the power used. If you can avoid having an operator, it will, of course, reduce the total considerably, although it may result in greater maintenance charges.

Remember that you must specify the speed with which the elevator is to travel. If doors open on one side only, operation is simplified, although it is possible to have doors on more than one side of the cab. Unless an elevator is a slow-moving one, problems will arise if you try to have it stop at an in-between level only a few feet above or below the one where it started. Elevators are often used to help solve the floor-level problem in an addition, when the levels in the new and the old sections do not match, and trouble in this connection may arise.

To go back to the problem of the required number of elevators, whether in banks or separated, the decision should be based on the time the library is prepared to have its patrons or its staff wait. If the building is only three levels high, most persons—when not engaged in carrying books up and down—can walk if they are in a hurry. But, as already indicated, people tend to be physically if not mentally lazy. They also tend to be impatient and do not want to wait even a minute for elevator service. If the elevator is used by staff members, the waiting minutes pile up, and the cost in staff time may be considerable. Elevator manufacturers have developed formulas on which the number of elevators required is based. They involve the time it takes a lift to go the full distance from one end of the shaft to the other and the time that should be allowed for slowing up for each stop, for opening the door, for getting the passengers out and in, for closing the door, and for getting started. (The deeper the cab and the narrower the door opening, the longer the time—other things being equal—a person will take to leave and enter.) The formulas show the maximum delay, with different numbers of cars, that can be expected before an elevator will be available.

Elevators today should ordinarily be wired for automatic push-button control because the cost of an operator is so great. The complicated controls which enable an elevator to do almost anything that you want it to and to memorize the calls that have been made, are much more satisfactory now than they were in earlier times when they tended to get out of order frequently.

One other elevator problem should be emphasized—noise. The machinery itself can be noisy. The same holds for doors. Fortunately, most elevator doors today slide back and forth and do not swing out, as some of those in the Widener Library

still do. The Widener doors make a heavy noise when allowed to slam. Since persons moving in groups tend to be noisy, do not place an elevator so that it opens into what should be a quiet reading room. The room will not stay quiet if you do. Acoustical protection will help, of course, but you must give it a fair chance.

Another warning. Be careful that elevators are placed so that their use will not interfere with a through traffic artery. Should an elevator open onto a main corridor, the lobby must be wide or there will be complications. The location is better just off a main corridor, but do not hide it unless you hope that the elevator will not be used.

If you do not have a booklift or an elevator, or even if you have one or more of both and they need to be supplemented, other types of mechanical transportation for books and for persons may be considered. These include levelators, escalators, endless belt conveyors, and pneumatic tubes.

In place of an elevator or booklift it is sometimes desirable to have a simple type of mechanical lift called a "levelator." Levelators are frequently seen in the sidewalks in business districts beside buildings with no shipping entrance and no loading dock. The levelator may be hidden under a sidewalk; when required, it rises so as to provide a loading dock. Heavy material can be shifted from a truck directly onto the levelator, and then transported down to a receiving room in the basement. Levelators can be very useful. One has been installed in an entirely different location at Harvard—at the Lamont end of the tunnel between the Houghton and the Lamont buildings, where the two floors to be connected are not the same level. Since rare books are carted back and forth, a steep ramp was unwise, so an inexpensive, and also noisy, levelator was installed at one end of the tunnel, outside the building. It has been very useful, and the noise does not disturb anyone in either building.

Escalators in libraries have been talked about for many years, but in public libraries only a few of them, to my knowledge, have been installed. In academic libraries, there is one at the Columbia Law School Library in New York, and a series of them in the library of the University of Miami in Coral Gables, Florida.

At Columbia, the entrance level of the building is used for large, amphitheater-like classrooms with high ceilings. To get up to the second floor where the library begins required a very long flight of stairs. An escalator seemed to be the solution. It has worked out satisfactorily, and the cost has not been unreasonable as it goes up only one flight in a straight run and does not have to be wide.

The installation at the University of Miami is also useful, but I think somewhat more questionable. It goes from the entrance lobby to the second floor by two runs, so as to take less space horizontally, and then has a third run from the second to the third floors. The second and third floors are smaller than the first floor in this library, so the number of people that go to the upper floors—while large—is not so great as it otherwise would be. The cost of escalators depends, of course, on the number of runs; whether there is one going both up and down between the floors which they connect; the square footage that they take on each of the floors, including the lobby space; the cost of the installation itself; and the cost of the operation and maintenance. The University of Miami decided to use the escalators because calculations indicated that the total cost amounted to less than that for four elevators which could not carry so many passengers. The question in my mind is whether as many as four elevators were needed. The Coral Gables escalators go *up* only until closing time, when they can be reversed.

I am sure that the use of escalators should be considered very carefully in any new building where there is need of transporting a large number of persons. It is difficult today, even in our very large libraries, to provide enough area on the entrance level to take care of the central services and a large number of readers, and many readers have to go to other levels. In the preliminary plans for a new library for New York University, where ground space is so expensive that the entrance level cannot be large enough to house the central services, it has been proposed that escalators should connect the entrance level with the second floor—where the central services would be installed—and also with the basement floor. With a larger area in the basement than on the floors above a tremendous number of seats would be provided here for an undergraduate reading room.

Do not forget about the possibility of escalators in large new buildings with heavy traffic between a limited number of floors. They may be noisy unless they are precision built; even then, they should be kept as far away as possible from what should be quiet reading areas. They do not need to run both up and down, but can be built so that at closing time the direction can be reversed, as at Coral Gables, and readers can be brought down from an upper level on the same escalator on which they went up earlier.

Endless belt conveyors have been used in libraries for the transportation of books at least since the beginning of the century. In the old building at the Library of Congress, they connected the bookstacks with the desk in the center of the main reading room. They were rather complicated in design, going up and down in the bookstacks, across through the basement, and then up to the desk. If my memory is correct, they were out of order from time to time, but they were, of course, far better than nothing. They are now being replaced. In the Harvard Law School Library, where the bookstacks

were in the lower floors, an endless belt conveyor carried books from the stacks up to the reading room on the top floor. This conveyor, also, became out of order and was very noisy; it was years before a way was found to quiet it.

A great many similar installations have been put into libraries in more recent years. The one at the Sterling Library at Yale, where the conveyor runs up and down through the stack tower and then across to the circulation desk, has been far from perfect but has had, of course, heavy use. The Widener Library, built in 1915, does not have an endless belt conveyor. The same was true of the New York Public Library's central building completed in 1911, as far as a vertical belt was concerned. But in the early twenties the booklifts there were replaced by endless belt conveyors of the simplest possible type, which ran only through the seven levels of the bookstacks to the reading room above. The books could be put on the conveyor at any stack level. They were taken up into the reading room where there was always an attendant waiting to deal with them. It is possible to construct a conveyor so that it can drop books off or pick them up at each level, but every added complication increases the tendency for it to get out of order. As far as I know, the conveyors in the New York Public Library have provided more satisfactory service than the more elaborate installations elsewhere.

Endless belt conveyors can involve noise, as has been mentioned in connection with the Harvard Law School installation. They can creak and groan, but there is no reason why there should be any serious complication of this kind today, particularly if the conveyors are properly located.

The question arises as to how the books should be carried. Vertical conveyors ordinarily have shelves connected with the endless belt at right angles. The books are dropped from those shelves mechanically into a chute. It is always undesirable to place books directly onto the shelf because there is danger of damage. They should be placed in an open, lightweight box of canvas or papier mache, which will prevent the books from dropping down the shaft as they are placed on the conveyor or when they leave it. The boxes also serve as added protection if a book that leaves the conveyor has not been taken away by an attendant before the next one appears on the scene. It is safer to have boxes with books in them bump into each other than to have books bump into each other. We all know the damage that results when books collide and knife each other in a night return box, and this is a similar situation. If conveyor-belt shelves are attached once in 15 feet or less, even if the belt goes at a slow rate of speed, the total capacity if larger than is required in a busy library stack in delivering books to a reading room. If you try to return the books from the reading room to the different stack levels in large numbers at one time by an endless belt conveyor, there may be delays as well as breakdowns due to complicated controls. I suggest that it is better to put books for return on a book truck and transport them by service elevator.

Conveyors should be large enough to carry fairly large-size books, or rather boxes that will hold large-size books. They should make as few turns as possible, particularly where it means a shifting from one vertical plane to another, because that is where complications tend to arise. On the other hand, it must be remembered that conveyors are being used more and more in industry, and undoubtedly better ones will be available year by year. In a heavily used multilevel stack they should be seriously considered.

There is a second type of endless belt conveyor which is used sometimes in a very large building, such as the New York Public Library—one to carry books horizontally instead of vertically. The experience at the New York Public Library has been that horizontal conveyors are more prone to get out of order than vertical ones. This may be because these particular conveyors were built a good many years earlier.

The time needed to carry books by comparatively slow-moving endless belt conveyors brings up the desirability of more rapid methods when a considerable distance is involved. This was the problem faced by the Library of Congress when the annex to the Library was built over twenty-five years ago. Pneumatic tubes were installed to carry books, just as pneumatic tubes have been used for years in large libraries to carry call slips from one part of the building to another.

As far as I know, the busiest of these pneumatic tube installations for call slips is in the New York Public Library, where as many as 5,000 or more slips may be transported in this way in one day. There is a central station inside the main reading room desk to which the call slips are carried by air pressure from stations all over the building, and from which they are sent on to the seven stack levels or to the various subject reading rooms. An expert operator handles slips with unbelievable speed, and the service on the whole has been fairly satisfactory although it has tended to be noisy. Fortunately, the stations are generally in places where the noise has not been a serious matter.

In the new Olin Library at Cornell, pneumatic tubes were installed to carry call slips back and forth between the circulation desk and the stacks, and a special problem arose. The call slips were IBM cards which were larger than the standard call slips and could not be bent or rolled. They required a larger container and for some time they tended to stick as they went around corners, but I understand that this tendency has now been corrected.

As noted earlier, not only call slips but books can be sent through pneumatic tubes. The Library of Congress wanted to transport books between its two buildings. In each basement there was a room where the books were placed in large containers and propelled by pneumatic pressure to the other building. A new problem arose. The containers rushed through the tubes built for the purpose at tremendous speeds, coming to a quick stop at the end of their journey. This meant that unless they were fastened very securely, the books were likely to be damaged by the sudden jar. To strap them in tightly enough tended to damage the bindings. This problem, I understand, has continued.

During the past few months, with the building of the new central research library at the University of California in Los Angeles, it was important to connect the old library and the new building—a distance of perhaps 600 feet. Pneumatic tubes were installed, and again the problem of damage to books had to be faced. Two methods have been worked out to help the situation. The tunnel through which the tubes pass runs underground to avoid obstructions, and at the end of the journey the books travel uphill a considerable distance. By shutting off the pressure on the uphill section, they are slowed up by the time they reach their destination. In addition, it has been found that if the books are held tightly with a large-size clamp, there is less possibility of damage than if they are strapped in.

I might have included other types of communications in this talk: telephones, intercoms, telautographs, teletype, public address systems, closed-circuit television, walkie-talkies, as well as various audio-visual aids. I could have presented a dissertation on book trucks or roller skates, to say nothing of automation. They are all in the picture, but I will content myself by saying: Be sure to plan your library with sufficient flexibility and wiring so that any or all of these installations will be possible without unnecessarily expensive alterations.

Discussion

Question: I would like to ask you if you have any opinions on the difference between those pneumatic tubes requiring a carrier and those which do not.

MR. METCALF: I understand Kansas City (Missouri) Public Library has one that does not require a carrier. The book just goes through it.

Question: I was talking about call slips.

MR. METCALF: I have no information on that point. Is someone here from Kansas City who can speak on this?

SPEAKER FROM THE FLOOR: I am from the library in Kansas City, and we do have a tube that handles cards only. The cards are carried by air through the tube. I have heard of no trouble with the system. It is working satisfactorily.

MR. METCALF: That is the same kind of installation the New York Public Library has, which I described to you.

Question: Will this system handle books?

MR. METCALF: The one at New York Public Library does not handle books.

Question: In a medium-sized library, where pneumatic tubes and that sort of thing are not needed, there is still the problem of transporting books upstairs. Is there any reason why an escalator could not be built with steps broad enough to hold a wheelchair, book truck, or anything else that needed to be transported up or down?

MR. METCALF: That would be possible, but if a book truck is 3 feet long, the flat step would have to be 3 feet long, and if you are going up, you would have a little difficulty getting on the escalator while it was traveling. In addition, the escalator would take about four times as much space, and space costs more money in the library than anything else. Possibly it is the thing to do but it would be expensive in space.

Question: Do you have any suggestions for writing specifications that would guarantee the best type of elevator and exclude those that are not so good?

MR. METCALF: As I said at the beginning of my discussion, I am not an engineer or an architect, and I certainly do not know enough about the technical details so that I could write specifications. I think you can find architects who can. Of course, you can get the elevator companies to do it, but they may be prejudiced.

Question: Dr. Metcalf, I would like to get your reaction to the usefulness of a maintenance contract with the elevator installer. If the elevator does not work, the contract should get you very quick service. If you disagree, I would be glad to hear your reaction to the idea.

MR. METCALF: I agree with you completely. I would always have a service contract in connection with almost any kind of mechanical installation in the library.

Question: If I may ask one other question: In my experience, when there are elevators in public libraries, one of the biggest problems is their abuse or misuse by youngsters and the continual ringing of call bells or emergency stop signals. This bothers our library, and I know that it has bothered others. I would be most appreciative for suggestions as to how this problem can be solved other than by using an operator.

MR. METCALF: This problem of abuse of library facilities is one that comes up in all aspects of library work. You may remember that Joe Wheeler almost suggests that libraries should have no toilet facilities because they tend to be abused. He has not quite committed himself to that extent. That misuse is part of the same overall problem. I read recently that the Brooklyn Public Library lost a half-million dollars' worth of books, or something of that sort, last year. This is another case. I wish I knew the solution.

In our college and university libraries, we have found that we have helped the situation in regard to book loss by checking people as they leave the building, making them show their brief cases. In other countries, precaution goes much further than that. If you go to almost any university library in the English-speaking world outside of the United States, you will not be allowed to bring your brief case into the building at all. You have to go in empty-handed and go out empty-handed. I remember going into a university library in Australia, where there was an entrance corridor 10 feet wide and 40 feet long. From that, you entered the library itself. You were not allowed to bring your brief case in. That entrance corridor was so full of brief cases that I could not get through it without walking over them. Well, the library was trying to solve its problem in that way. If any of you have other suggestions, I would be glad to have them.

Question: I would appreciate it very much if you would say a few words on the need for telephones and intercommunications systems in college libraries.

MR. METCALF: This is a very difficult problem to deal with in a few words, I can assure you. I am inclined to think that if the telephones you have can be adjusted so that you can call someone else in the library without having to call an operator, it will save you considerable time. Telephones can be very expensive in a college library. In the first draft of the book I am doing on college library building planning, I said that telephones were abused in libraries because even college professors sometimes used them for long-distance calls when the phones were not supervised. I was told that this was insulting. I have taken the statement out of my book, and perhaps I should not mention it here. Nevertheless, to leave a telephone unattended anywhere can be serious. Sometimes it is better to arrange to have the phones disconnected at night when a person leaves or a desk is closed, so that they cannot be used without authorization. Sometimes you can put the telephone in a cupboard and lock it up. On the other hand, telephones are almost a necessity in conducting the business of a library. There was a tendency a good many years ago to have library telephone installations separate from the telephone company's installations. In the Oberlin College library that was finished in 1908, we had, in the librarian's office, telephone connections with all rooms in the building. The system was always out of order. Soon it was given up, and the standard type of telephone put into use.

The Carpeted Library

JOE B. GARRETT
Director of Merchandising
American Carpet Institute
New York City, New York

The growing list of carpeted libraries indicates that librarians are well aware of library flooring requirements and, especially, of the ability of soft floor coverings, such as carpeting, to contribute economically to the solution of some library environmental problems of long standing.

To the user, a library is a retreat where he can find information quickly and study it in relative quiet. Next to adequate selection and quick location of information, the physical make-up of the library is probably the most important requirement from the user's point of view. By physical make-up I mean adequate acoustical and visual privacy, which are noted in the conscious mind of the library user only when acoustics are obviously inferior or when he is constantly distracted visually.

Even the casual library patron knows that library planning has been intensified in recent years, much as all academic planning and facilities have received concentrated attention. In the view of many, the library has come to serve as the barometer of interest in knowledge, particularly so with the great emphasis being placed on individual inquiry and study as important phases of school programs.

The library is subject to more, and in many cases different, kinds of use today than ever before. And with new use and new attention has come the upgrading of interior elements which combine to produce an effective environment. In short, library planners have risen to the occasion.

From the outsider's point of view, this upgrading seems to have been accelerated by an apparent "breaking out of the mold," which has meant a broadening of the library's scope and function, its fulfillment of a teaching instrument role, and a shedding of its more-or-less traditional, study hall image. It has meant, too, the incorporation, in varying degrees, of audio-visual and a range of other mechanical devices which tend to be noise-producing, thereby creating the need for careful acoustical planning. What I have stated is simply a review of the reasons behind the rapid trend toward carpeted libraries.

Carpet fits well into modern library requirements. Its basic character offers the benefits of beauty, dignity, and ease of care, but the compelling reason for its use in libraries is its ability to serve as a superior acoustical material at the floor level. This fact is quickly accepted.

Everybody understands that the library should be quiet—not tomblike, but certainly free of extraneous and unnecessary noise. Carpets deliver this needed quiet by eliminating floor-instigated or impact noise such as foot shuffling, dropping of books and pencils, and the moving of desks and chairs, while psychologically dignifying and creating user respect and positive behavior patterns. These advantages have put carpet in the common-sense category as a library floor covering.

The carpeted library, whether a private or a public institution, is seldom controversial any more. The trend to carpet was not stimulated artificially but originated with administrators, architects, and planners who looked for and found a floor covering with performance qualities that would meet the needs of modern design trends in libraries.

The Library Technology Project report on the use of carpeting in libraries indicates that its use is increasing. The report cites its superior acoustical properties, lower maintenance costs, vast improvement in decor, and the immediate and positive psychological effects as experienced by the Arcadia (California) Public Library; the University of South Carolina Library, the reading rooms of which were first carpeted as early as 1840; and a number of other school and public libraries.[1]

The Educational Facilities Laboratories, in its school library report, points to Foothill College, Los Altos, California; Kansas City (Missouri) Public Library; and Andrews (Texas) High School Library as three which have solved severe acoustical problems by using carpet. This report also points to reduced maintenance costs—the savings from which are substantial over the carpet's wear life.[2]

Recently the Educational Facilities Laboratories published a study on acoustical environment of school buildings by architect John Lyon Reid and acoustical expert Dariel Fitzroy. Two carpeted schools with carpeted libraries were reported as being acoustically superior with an overwhelmingly excellent rating from teachers and tests.[3] Later, at

1. American Library Association, Library Technology Project, "The Use of Carpeting in Libraries" (Chicago: American Library Assn., 1962). 12p. Mimeographed.
2. Ralph E. Ellsworth and Hobart D. Wagener, *The School Library: Facilities for Independent Study in the Secondary School* (New York: Educational Facilities Laboratories, Inc., 1963).
3. Dariel Fitzroy and John Lyon Reid, *Acoustical Environment of School Buildings* (New York: Educational Facilities Laboratories, Inc., 1963).

a news conference sponsored by the American Carpet Institute, following the publication of the report, coauthor of the study Dariel Fitzroy stated: "Carpets in the corridors and classrooms of schools may become an essential fundamental in the planning of schools in the immediate future. In the light of modern school requirements, carpeting gives evidence of being a necessity."

Dr. Harold Gores, President of Educational Facilities Laboratories, writing in the *Nation's Schools*, had this to say:

"Studies of comparative costs tend to show that over the long haul of the years, carpeting will save money, especially if all factors are included—lower maintenance costs; possibility of reducing the number of partitions that would otherwise have to be constructed; likelihood of reduction in fuel consumption (estimated by L. P. Herrington at 5%); increase in reflected light from ceilings no longer designed around sound absorption; reduction of micro-organisms floating in the air; and the greatest factor of all—though probably immeasurable except by testimony—the effect on the student's morale and how he feels about the place in which he works.

"But whether carpeting is cheaper is not the central question. What is central is whether an acoustic floor covering will help children to see better, hear better, act better, and learn more. An increasing number of educators believe this to be the case."[4]

The acoustical properties of carpeting were first measured, in 1955, by Dr. Cyril Harris of Columbia University, now President of the Acoustical Society of America. The ability of carpeting to act as a noise absorbent was rated at .55 and interpreted as being as effective as most materials designed specifically for the purpose of noise reduction.[5]

Dr. Harris also found that carpet absorbed ten times the amount of airborne noise as other types of floor coverings (examples being voice or machine noise) and that it virtually eliminated impact noises (clattering of heels, moving of chairs and desks, and dropping of materials). These findings were confirmed in field tests by Professors Rodman and Kunz of Rensselaer Polytechnic Institute who conducted tests in the carpeted Shaker High School, Newtonville, New York—the first school to use carpet for acoustical and maintenance cost-reduction purposes. They also commented on the good sense of *eliminating* floor-instigated noises in this manner rather than allowing the noises to be created and then trying to trap them with acoustical materials on other room surfaces.

In carpeted areas, large dollar savings can often be realized by eliminating other acoustical treatments. This elimination is an advantage for libraries, since the ceilings must no longer be designed around noise-control materials and can be used for the most desirable lighting. Subsequent acoustical studies and observations, particularly in the educational field, have repeatedly drawn attention to the desirability of the acoustical floor covering.

What do the tests on maintenance show? About nine years ago a maintenance cost study conducted by Industrial Sanitation Counselors, an independent housekeeping consultant firm for some of the nation's leading corporations and hotels, established that carpet was easier and substantially cheaper to maintain than hard floors under conditions of heavy, medium, and light traffic.[6] Over the years this evidence has mounted.

As late as last year, a new and broadened maintenance study conducted by the same firm showed that carpet's total-use cost—including its initial and maintained cost, averaged over its life—was about one half the cost of other floor coverings. The actual total-use cost of 1,000 square feet of carpet compared to the same area of traditional tile floors was $182.41 for carpet, $348.29 for tile.

The booklet *Cutting Costs with Carpet*, which contains full details of these studies, is available free of charge from the American Carpet Institute, 350 Fifth Avenue, New York, New York 10001.

A number of reports from librarians have appeared, based on actual field experience, stating that these estimates of maintenance savings are actually somewhat conservative. Among these is the report on Foothill College, mentioned earlier. Obviously, no mopping, stripping, waxing, buffing, rewaxing, and the like are needed. Large maintenance savings are realized through lower expenditures for labor, capital equipment, and expendable supplies. Carpeting is simply far easier and less costly to maintain at a much higher appearance level. It affords scientific maintenance, which too few people practice.

It has been my observation, in talking with professionals, that these maintenance figures are looked upon with skepticism only by those who have not had direct experience with carpeted schools or libraries. Quite impressive validation of these figures is supplied by a recently established company on the West Coast which some of you may know. This organization contracts with schools to take over total floor maintenance at the figure currently being paid by the school for this service. The con-

4. Reprinted, with permission, from Harold B. Gores, "Some Factors That Affect Future Schoolhouse Planning," *Nation's Schools*, 65:74-77 (April 1960). Copyright, 1960, The Modern Hospital Publishing Co., Inc., Chicago.
5. Cyril M. Harris, "Acoustical Properties of Carpet," *Journal of the Acoustical Society of America*, 27:1077-82 (Nov. 1955).

6. *Cutting Costs with Carpet*; a study by Industrial Sanitation Counselors, Inc., Louisville, Kentucky (New York: American Carpet Institute, 1956).

tract stipulates that carpeting will be supplied by the company and installed throughout the school at no charge to the school itself. The company's profits are then realized through a substantial reduction in current floor maintenance costs. The school pays no more and has carpet installed and properly maintained—free of charge.

Let me give you a few specific examples of schools using carpet. Shaker High School, Newtonville, New York, has 25,000 square feet of carpet in academic areas. Now in the seventh year of use, the results have been unbelievably favorable. The library lounge is carpeted and provides an ideal area for relaxation and study. The floor is used as a work area. There is obviously an advantage in this increased utilization of space. Students do not object to sitting, editing a yearbook, or holding entire classes on carpeted floors. Shaker High School physics classes use carpeted stair risers as classroom seats.

Millard Smith, principal of the school, says:

"The noise of a school is impact noise: footsteps, foot shuffling, the scraping of chairs and desks on the floor, the dropping of books and pencils. Carpeting is the only flooring material that absorbs impact noises sufficiently so that they are barely heard.... Carpeting contributes significantly to the de-institutionalizing of the school and school life. Students take greater pride in the school and are more relaxed in the activities they carry on there. The presence of carpet has been observed by all of our faculty as a major cause of positive habit development by students using these areas. There is a unanimous feeling on the part of the staff that they would prefer to teach in carpeted rooms. Because the atmosphere is informal, the teachers at Shaker find it easier to develop a close relationship between student and teacher."

The library of the Andrews (Texas) High School contains 45,000 square feet of carpet in the academic areas. Comments on this library environment have been extremely favorable. Architect John Lyon Reid was able, in this case, to use the ceiling for completely luminous lighting, rather than for acoustical purposes, because he believed that adequate acoustical treatment had been applied at the floor level.

The Morton High School library in Cicero, Illinois, also illustrates the improved lighting and some of the color and design advantages of carpeted floors. Longwood High School, Middle Island, New York, has used carpet for some time with results that have been particularly gratifying. The Moses Brown School, Providence, Rhode Island, is another example of the effective use of color in library planning with good quality carpet. In this and other libraries the anticipated problem of rolling heavy book trucks over carpet has, in most cases, simply not presented itself. In other cases, special 6-inch

by $1\frac{1}{2}$-inch plastic casters have been used, as recommended by the Library Technology Project.

The Jesuit School in Dallas, Texas, used both carpet and acoustical tile for noise-control purposes. The Brazosport High School, Freeport, Texas, is a modern library both in design and in furnishings. It uses a carpeting beige in color with a tweed texture. Almost any color seems suitable today. People seem to expect more unusual library colors. Specifications will naturally vary somewhat according to end use and type and amount of traffic.

Finally, let me mention the Beinecke Rare Book Library at Yale University, which utilizes a vast expanse of carpeting. In this library glass wall partitions are used to separate various areas of the library. Noise from traffic on one side of the glass wall would be highly distracting were there no carpet to muffle the sound.

The libraries I have mentioned are representative of several hundred which are carpeted today. We at the Institute hear about a great many more as each week passes. I might also mention the relationship between the carpeted library and the carpeted hospital, although it may be obvious to you. Hospitals, at a very rapid rate, are now using carpet for acoustical and maintenance purposes and with excellent results. Tests are being conducted at the carpeted Barnes Hospital in St. Louis to determine correct maintenance procedures and methods. Preliminary studies at the Genesee Hospital in Rochester, New York, have indicated a lower germ count in carpeted areas than in uncarpeted. This phase is still being studied. The St. Louis University Library also has considerable carpeting in a large lounge area.

To conclude, here are the practical advantages of carpeting in libraries:

All room surfaces considered, it costs no more, or very little more, initially
The highly favorable maintenance record compared with that of other floor coverings reduces costs and allows for replacement at the same time that a much higher appearance level is maintained
Acoustical treatment on the floor will likely allow ceilings to be designed for improved lighting
Carpet creates a respectable, workable, upgraded library environment which, in turn, creates respect on the part of the user
Carpet can be used more quickly and economically as a replacement floor covering in older libraries to bring them completely up to date. It is the only deployable floor covering—removable, reshapable, reusable
Carpet controls noise at the floor level, where troublesome library noise originates

Resilient Flooring Materials in Libraries

GEORGE F. JOHNSTON
Marketing Manager
Armstrong Cork Company
Lancaster, Pennsylvania

First, I want to express my own appreciation and that of the Armstrong Cork Company for the opportunity to be with you this evening. We have been hearing from many sources of your interest in the question of which is the best floor for a library. In the next few minutes I hope I can underline a few considerations that may not have come to your attention.

Rather than try to draw comparisons between the many types of floors and floor coverings available to you, I am going to concentrate on the facts surrounding the use of resilient floors and let you make your own comparisons based on these facts. For details, I shall be referring to Armstrong materials, but this offers no limitations to my story; we have been making floors for more than sixty years, and today our product line covers the full range of resilient flooring materials. Armstrong sheet floors include both linoleum and vinyl. In addition, we make every type of tile: cork, rubber, vinyl, linoleum, asphalt, and vinyl-asbestos. We offer this broad selection because we have learned over the years that no single flooring material is universally right for every job. Individual tastes and job requirements have become too specific and diversified, and only a floor designed and manufactured to meet specific needs can fill the bill.

How do you select a floor? I see at least six separate factors that must be weighed in a flooring decision; how you rate them in importance for your own use will determine which floor you should choose:

1. *Design.* Since some flooring materials offer greater design opportunities than others, your own taste and preferences will affect the choice of basic material
2. *Durability.* One building or floor area will demand greater wear resistance than another, so that variations among the different types of materials must be weighed in the decision
3. *Maintenance.* Janitorial schedules and techniques vary, and the floor selected must be able to retain its good appearance under the particular maintenance level it will receive
4. *Sanitation.* Here you must take into account who will use the room and the amount of dirt and dust the floor will collect. While resilient floors as a group do not retain dust, your sani-

tation requirements could determine whether or not other materials should be considered
5. *Resilience.* Since even resilient floors differ among themselves in the underfoot comfort and quietness they offer, this can be a critical factor in your selection
6. *Cost.* Varied combinations of performance and appearance features are available for the amount of money you have to spend

Obviously, these six factors can be applied not only to resilient floors, but to the whole range of floors and floor coverings you may consider. Those of you responsible for selecting the floor for a new or remodeled library will have to seek the right balance of qualities for your job, at the right price, and with the most economical maintenance outlook. We recognize that other materials outside our line can sometimes present the best solution for a particular area. Resilient floors occupy a median position—midway between the hardest and the softest flooring surfaces. That is why we believe they come closest to being the universal floor for buildings with a considerable degree of foot traffic. Our goal is simply to provide as much as the capabilities of our materials and manufacturing methods will allow to give you the widest possible choice within the median position we occupy.

In the past, resilient floors—both tile and sheet goods—earned acceptance chiefly by virtue of their practical advantages. They offered the commercial and institutional building long wear at a relatively low cost; easy cleanability of foot traffic and stains; and a quieter permanent surface than the wood and terrazzo floors that were the previous standard. Over the years, these original maintenance advantages have been improved still further. New equipment and techniques have cut cleaning and waxing time; new vinyl materials have their own natural gloss; and the development of commercial self-polishing waxes has largely eliminated the need for buffing.

But, today, maintenance is only part of the story. Another factor has begun to influence many decisions in favor of resilient floors—their vastly improved styling. The development of vinyl as a flooring material and the application of new technology have allowed us to manufacture more attractive designs, colors, textures, and dimensional effects. This flexibility has broadened the whole spectrum of possible designs, so that we are now better able to create specific styles to appeal to the homeowner, and others to meet the needs of public buildings. Architects and interior designers today have the wider choice they have asked for in color and surface texture, along with new opportunities to create custom-design effects to complement the overall function and decor of an interior.

All these factors have helped to make resilient floors the current standard for offices, schools,

	INSTALLED COST PER SQ. FT.	RESILIENCE	DURABILITY	STAIN RESISTANCE	EASE OF MAINTENANCE
SHEET FLOORS					
Vinyl Corlon	.70– 1.15	4	2	1	2
Linoleum	.45– .55	4	3	4	3
TILE FLOORS					
Vinyl Corlon	2.30–3.60	5	1	1	2
Vistelle Corlon	1.90–2.00	1	1	1	2
Custom Vinyl Cork	1.75– 1.85	3	4	1	1
Custom Corlon	.80– 1.15	2	1	1	2
Linotile	.75– .80	5	1	2	1
Standard Cork	.60– .95	1	5	5	5
Rubber	.60– .70	2	2	2	3
Excelon	.35– .40	6	2	4	2
Asphalt	.15– .30	7	3	5	4

Figure 16
Characteristics of resilient tile floors

hospitals, and stores—any building or room where wear and maintenance factors are as important as appearance. I will be covering these advantages in more depth as I go along. But, first, I want to give you a broad picture of just how resilient floors are now being used in the type of building you are concerned with—libraries. All of the factors I have listed—design, durability, maintenance, sanitation, resilience, and cost—are being tested in the best laboratories we know—the libraries themselves.

Now let us review some of the factors that influence the choice of a resilient floor. Figure 16 shows each type of resilient floor we make, along with its approximate installed cost per square foot and the relative rating of these materials in four performance areas: resilience, durability, stain resistance, and ease of maintenance. The figure 1 represents top performance; the figure 5, relatively poor performance. I will not try to analyze all these variations in detail, but I do want to emphasize the fact that these performance variations exist and that they must be weighed in making your choice. Our published technical data for architects include more factors than those shown here: for example, the floor's relative resistance to heel damage, cigarette burns, grease, and alkali. Some of these many factors will be important in your specifications; others will not. You must analyze these facts and then decide what qualities are most important to you.

Let me illustrate. One of our new materials, Vistelle Corlon, is made from Dupont Hypalon, a synthetic with an unusual combination of physical properties. It is the best all-around performer in our line, with top ratings in resilience, durability, and stain resistance, and one of the easiest floors to maintain. But it also costs about $2 a square foot installed, so that for some building budgets it might have to be limited to high-traffic entrance foyers or around the check-out desk. Its design and colorings are geared to the more subtle requirements of institutional interiors. If you want this kind of styling but cannot afford Vistelle, then the next step down the price ladder, with similar styling, is Imperial Custom Corlon. This is a homogeneous vinyl tile in the range of $1 a square foot. Its durability is on the same high level with Vistelle, but with a slightly lesser degree of resilience and resistance to stains. If your budget is still squeezed at this figure, you can get almost identical styling in Imperial Rubber Tile at 60¢ to 70¢ an installed foot. The only step-down in quality is in the area of grease resistance, which would not be significant in your specifications.

Rubber tile is a popular choice for libraries, since it is one of the quietest floors in the medium-priced group. In the same price range is Dorelle Corlon, a vinyl sheet material that provides similar subdued styling and colors but with the maintenance and appearance advantages of a virtually seamless floor. Thus, another factor enters the decision—tile or sheet goods.

At the bottom of the price scale you can choose from designs in asphalt and vinyl-asbestos tile products—in the range of 20¢ to 40¢ a square foot installed. Durability and ease of maintenance closely match the more expensive floors, but with a sacrifice of resilience and quietness—both very important factors in your decision.

Now let me take another approach. Say that you are interested in just one or two specific qualities above all others. For example, that you want the best floor for durability and ease of maintenance. The top performer in these two categories is Linotile, a product somewhat similar to linoleum but cured longer to increase its durability. Its long wear and easy cleaning are a direct result of the material's hardness, so that it is necessary to compromise on the degree of quietness underfoot. Suppose you want the quietest resilient tile available. Vistelle, the top all-around performer, is one choice. Another would be standard cork tile with equally high resilience at a lower cost. But cork tile, due to its natural porosity, is less durable and requires more maintenance than other resilient tiles; so for those who prefer the natural appearance of cork but do not want to sacrifice good maintenance features, cork tiles with a heavy vinyl surface are the answer. They rate right up with Linotile in case of maintenance, with only a moderate decrease in resilience from natural cork. The vinyl coating has also allowed us to do more in the way of design.

One more example. Suppose that you have decided to give a certain area—such as a memorial reading room—the best in styling and design but at the same time are concerned about the effect of women's stiletto heels on your floor. Here you can take two approaches. You might select from a design in vinyl tile, which offers the best in design while simultaneously giving almost complete resistance to heel damage. Or, you can choose from designs in vinyl sheet goods: Montina and Tessera Corlon. The same three-dimensional surface that gives them their design appeal also acts to camouflage any spike-heel marks that occur. Of course, the range in styling and colors goes far beyond what I have discussed here. My point is that even though resilient floors generally are easy to maintain and wear well, there are variations among the various types that you should consider carefully.

Now that I have pointed out how various resilient floors differ among themselves, let us think about them as a group, specifically in regard to practical considerations. As I said earlier, resilient floors have gained their wide acceptance primarily for two practical reasons: durability and ease of maintenance, qualities they have demonstrated conclusively over many years. But some persons have reached the conclusion that libraries do not require such a high degree of performance; that the advantages soft-surface floor coverings provide in underfoot comfort and quietness offset the necessity to replace them more often; and that the lower maintenance cost of these coverings compensates for the expense of their replacement.

It is true that libraries are quiet places, but they are also the scene of much activity. Their floors must withstand the dirt tracked in from the outdoors; they must absorb punishment from the constant use of book trucks; and in some areas, such as aisles and corridors, they are subject to relatively heavy foot traffic. In fact, in many ways this activity is much closer to that of a supermarket than the level of sound would infer. The floors must be able to take this punishment every day, must be economically maintained to your standards of cleanliness, and must hold that appearance for many years.

I do not think that I have to go into any detail about the fact that resilient floors are the best answer to these practical requirements. The only facts that seem to have become confused are those relating to the cost of maintenance. Remember that the maintenance cost figures meaningful to you are those that relate to the specific type of flooring material you have, the degree of cleanliness you desire, and the janitorial methods and schedules that will be applied to do the job.

For example, I understand that an organization serving government buildings in Washington, D.C., requires that the asphalt tile be swept daily and waxed four times a year. The cost for this maintenance is a yearly average of 17¢ a square foot. The carpets and rugs are vacuumed an average of two and one-half times a week and shampooed twice a year. The annual cost for this is 45¢ a square foot—two and one-half times the figure for asphalt tile.

Your library may have a cork tile floor that requires twice as much waxing, or a rubber tile floor that requires less. You may want your carpet vacuumed more often or less often, depending on the kind of traffic you get or the appearance standard you require. On resilient floors, the maintenance cost will depend on the type of equipment used, the janitorial pay scale in your area, and whether or not you use self-polishing wax. All I am saying is that when you start to compare maintenance costs, be sure the figures relate to the specific type of floors you are considering and the degree of maintenance you intend to give them.

I listed sanitation as a separate factor from maintenance, mainly because there is a significant difference between a floor that looks clean and one that is really clean and sanitary from a health standpoint. Many of you operate libraries for young children, and I know you must carefully consider not just the greater wear and dirt children's feet bring with them, but the need for a relatively dust-free atmosphere. Since allergies and hay fever are common causes of school absenteeism among young children, there is a great advantage in a floor that will not catch and retain dust and dirt and allow it to be reintroduced into the room. I am sure your local authorities can supply you with specific information on the special regular care required for draperies, rugs, and upholstered furniture to keep them free from dust and allergens.

I have covered considerable ground in a few minutes, but I hope you can now see that this job of specifying a floor is one of the more complex decisions on interior finish materials you must make. We are prepared to help you in every way we can to make the right decision for your needs, whether it be for a specialized area or for an entire building. In every major city we have architect-builder-consultants who are specialists in large flooring specifications; and, of course, our representatives who work with our wholesalers and retailers are available for consultation at any point in the country. Not only can these men supply the technical information you need on various materials; they can also recommend the most effective, economical means of maintaining them.

Should you require more detailed technical assistance or have an unusual installation problem, we offer the services of our Research and Development Center in Lancaster, Pennsylvania, with its extensive test data and experiences in all types of installations. As for the choice of color and design, our interior design studio—also in Lancaster—can recommend resilient floors that will best suit the atmosphere and style of your building, working within your practical and budgetary requirements. In other words, we want you to have the right floor—one that will make a positive, long-lasting contribution to your operation.

Flooring Materials for Libraries— A Panel Discussion

Moderator:
FRANK E. GIBSON
Director
Omaha Public Library
Omaha, Nebraska

Panel Members:
CHARLES DALRYMPLE
Librarian
Bennett Martin Public Library
Lincoln, Nebraska

HOMER L. FLETCHER
City Librarian
Arcadia, California

ALFRED RAWLINSON
Director of Libraries
McKissick Memorial Library
University of South Carolina
Columbia, South Carolina

JOAN SHINEW
Librarian
Colorado College
Colorado Springs, Colorado

CHARLES DALRYMPLE

In our new building, which was opened in October, 1962, we have a complete carpeting installation on both floors, including all service areas, the assembly room of the children's department, and the work areas. In planning the building, we took the first step of total design and tried to incorporate all those details necessary to create an environment that would accomplish the purposes described in our program. We felt that the interior, which would be exposed to the public view from the outside and would be a very large open area—in fact, we have very few partition walls—would be best suited to a carpet installation.

Our decision was guided by the principle of trying to determine what would make the most suitable environment for the library patron. I am speaking about a public library installation, and I would like to emphasize that in public libraries one of the problems is how to deal with the heavy student use. We have less concern about fixed or scheduled activities and constant occupancy—that is, people who stay in the library continually. In fact, I would say that 90 percent of our traffic is "in and out."

One of our first concerns was to obtain a flooring material that would facilitate the movement of people to the books and to the desk. The plan, of course, required an atmosphere of calm and quiet, as well as an attractive place in which to examine the books in the collection. We also gave considerable thought to the casual areas and to the lounge furniture. (Tables are relatively unimportant as visiting places.) Since we wanted to facilitate the flow of people around the books, we placed many of the bookstacks in open areas. We placed all our furniture on top of the carpeting. Although we have had occasion to move it several times, it has not yet created any marks on the carpeting.

Now let me point out some of the features of our installation that have not been stressed by others in the more general discussion. We like the acoustical qualities of carpeting and we like the pattern. Also, we like the fact that we have no glare spots on the floor from our lighting. This is an important factor when the library has a number of glass walls. We have an interior court that admits a great deal of sunlight, but the floors do not reflect this.

The atmosphere of calm and quiet produced by our carpeting seems to have a beneficial effect on both adults and young patrons. Previously, although we had a building with only half the floor space, there was a fairly constant commotion. Much of this was caused by our terrazzo and hard-surfaced floors. As a result, we wanted a material in the new building that would reduce floor noise.

In using carpeting in the assembly room and children's room areas, we were conscious of the fact that at times we would have large groups in the library and we might want to tell stories and have the children seated on the floor. We found the carpeting very successful when the children exceeded the number of cushions we had for them. We bought forty-eight cushions initially but they have not been enough, so we have used the floor on many occasions.

The psychological advantages of carpeting to the staff are hard to measure, but I do know that working conditions are very pleasant and that the staff enjoys the carpeting. One further note: After a year and a half, we have had no negative comments about our carpet. It is a pleasure not only to those who first see it, but to those who have used it since we opened.

HOMER L. FLETCHER

The Arcadia Public Library has been open to the public since April, 1961. Since that date patrons have crossed our threshold an estimated 500,000 times per year, or approximately 1,500,000 times in the three years we have been open. The carpet at the entry has borne all of this traffic at one spot, as we have only one public entrance and exit to the building; yet even this area is holding up very well and will not need replacement until some years hence.

Our decision to use carpeting in the Arcadia Public Library was not a hasty one. Numerous contacts were made with maintenance personnel, department stores, vinyl suppliers, public library maintenance staffs, carpet suppliers, carpet cleaners, and others. Recommendations as to types of flooring, including types of carpet, were requested from many sources. My list of contacts numbered about thirty individuals, firms, and institutions. Letters of information were solicited. When all this material was compiled, the following facts were evident:

Carpeting is 30-50 percent less costly to maintain than are hard floor coverings. The actual figures are about 25¢ per square foot annually, even with daily vacuuming, as compared to about 50¢ per square foot in the old building with resilient tile

Savings realized from lower maintenance expenditures will more than pay for replacement costs. The advance figures projected 4.3 pay-out years, or a 23.1 percent on our investment. Our actual experience has shown that this figure has been decreased to about 3.4 pay-out years with a 30 percent return on our investment

Carpeting is such a good sound conditioner that acoustical tile can be reduced or eliminated, depending on the ceiling design. For maximum sound control most experts recommend leaving the tile in, but if you need to show a savings here to get the carpet, omit it

The possibility of accidents is reduced

Carpeting is more comfortable underfoot than other floor coverings

Carpeting adds a feeling of warmth and enhances the general library atmosphere

The best possible specifications should be written so that the carpet installation will hold up under the closest inspection. Our findings showed an all-wool, loop pile, permanently moth-proofed, .250-inch pile height, commercial carpet to be our best choice. Our specifications, as finally written, were met exactly by Bigelow Gropoint. An all-hair pad was selected because this type does not stain carpeting in the event of water damage, whereas a dyed jute pad will stain.

The cost on the original bid was $11.85 per square yard in place, including a 40-ounce, all-hair felt pad with clamp-down metal at all exposed edges. We used carpeting every place where it was feasible —a total of 24,000 square feet. The shelving was set directly on top of the carpeting.

A few other points which I would like to mention as a result of our experience are:

Carpeting can be plugged and replaced if necessary

Spotting kits are available for removing motor oil, tar, and other substances

Shampooing has been needed less frequently than we originally thought. We now estimate every three to four years in public areas; every five to six years in office areas. Incidentally, wool will come back to a better appearance after a shampooing than other types of carpeting

The possibility of staining from the pad may be tested by soaking the sample in water overnight

The problem of static electricity is minor

The movement of book trucks is somewhat more difficult but presents no real problem

Damage from stacks is minor. When stacks have been moved, we cannot tell where they were prior to the move

I am so completely convinced of the advantages of carpeting over other types of floor coverings that I do not hesitate to recommend its use without reservation. Our three years of experience have only strengthened this belief.

ALFRED RAWLINSON

I am pleased to have this opportunity to give you a brief, nontechnical, consumer report on our experience with and reactions to wall-to-wall carpeting as a floor covering for major public areas of the libraries at the University of South Carolina. In our undergraduate library, which opened in the fall of 1959, there are approximately 2,400 square yards of such carpeting; and the main reading room of the University of South Carolina Library—an area of approximately 300 square yards—was covered with wall-to-wall carpeting two years after our initial installation had proved so eminently satisfactory.

The earliest extant picture of the first separate college library building in the United States, built in 1840—the one now known as the South Caroliniana Library on the campus of the University of South Carolina—shows wall-to-wall carpeting. Unfortunately, even though the full cycle has been traversed, and we are looking again at this type of floor covering for college libraries, no records of this initial installation can be located. It would be helpful to know the cost, durability, and experience with this 1840 installation, but it was no longer in use when I first entered the building in the early 1930's, and there are no records on it.

The genesis of the idea for the use of carpeting in the undergraduate library and the selection of the color came from the associate architect, Mr. Edward D. Stone. I would like briefly to describe our installation, to summarize our experience with it, and to make two suggestions of what we might do differently if we were faced with the same situation again.

First, as to the installation. Our chief engineer insisted that all concrete floors, both those to be carpeted and those which would remain bare in the storage area, receive a coat of regular floor sealer, although original plans for the building did not call for it. This sealing reduces the problem caused from dust created by lime in the concrete, which results in tracking when persons walk over bare concrete and then enter carpeted areas. Also, this same dust under the carpet would create a cleaning problem because vacuum cleaners tend to pull the dust up through the padding and carpet.

The specifications for our installation read:

"Carpet shall be attached to the concrete floor with tack strip. Griptac shall be used in doorways. Carpet shall be seamed with Kwik-Grip tape with steel pins every three inches. Rug Sealz cement shall be used to bond tape to carpet. Carpet cushion shall be 40-ounce 100% animal hair. Carpet shall be installed covering entire area called for on drawings, and book-shelves and other equipment or furniture will be installed or placed over carpet."

The actual carpet specifications were: surface yarns composed of 100 percent wool, round wire, woven through to the back, and complying with construction specifications of the National Carpet Institute as follows:

Pitch	216	Wire, per inch	8
Shot	2	Wire size	.250
		Ply wool	3

The rug we used was a needle-point weave which contributed to the durability. Cost of the complete installation was approximately $9.50 per square yard, which is not out of line with cost of quality floor covering of whatever nature.

Secondly, let me review our experience with carpeting over the past five years. Most of the following were areas of apprehension at the time of the installation and we could get no assurance from the experience of others. I am pleased to advise that our reservations have all proved to be groundless.

Mobility and tracking by book trucks have not been problems, though standard equipment is used. Static electricity generated by a person's walking on the carpet and then making contact with metal doorknobs has not been a problem, although such a condition develops to a mild degree when the humidity control occasionally becomes inoperative. The building is completely air-conditioned with controlled humidity. I understand that it is possible to have carpet treated chemically to avoid generation of static electricity, but we have not needed this.

From our one ink spill we have learned two things: (1) to remove an ink stain, professional service from an authorized carpet cleaner is necessary, and this must be done before the ink dries; (2) when cleaning fails, a piece of carpet can be removed and replaced. This can be done successfully by experts, and afterward the replacement is in no way noticeable. A reasonable supply of additional carpet should be purchased originally to provide for such an emergency.

The university's chief engineer advises me that he would estimate the cost of cleaning carpeted areas at 50 percent of that for other types of floor covering. The cleaning includes daily vacuuming plus annual shampoo, with a shampoo every six months in heavy traffic areas.

We have seen no evidence of fading due to sunlight exposure. Markings from furniture legs, apparent upon moving of the furniture, have not been a problem. The only evidence of wear, so far, has been on the edge of the stair treads, and the desirability of reducing noise in the open stairwell would make occasional replacement at this spot worth the cost. We believe that the carpet in the undergraduate library has been most successful as a means of reducing noise caused by walking, talking, and chair shuffling; as a means of reducing airborne dusts; for its aesthetic appeal; and as a psychological factor of importance.

If the same situation were faced again, I would make two recommendations: First, the areas of heavy use around the charging desk and the card catalog should receive a different type of floor covering. These areas accumulate dirt rather rapidly—in fact, they act almost as a front doormat—and hence require special attention at cleaning time.

Second, I would like to install, at all entrances, Miracle Mats as made by the Progressive Engineering Company of Holland, Michigan. This mat is a heavy aluminum grill, rubber-mounted, set within a welded steel frame installed in the floor. Brushes run the width of the grill just below the slats. The pressure of a footstep depresses the grill, activating limit switches and an electric motor which puts the brushes in motion. The brushes sweep up through the grill opening, back and forth, hundreds of strokes per minute, and keep on scrubbing shoe soles and heels until the pedestrian steps off the mat. Dirt may be carried away through dust collection systems or by flushing into the building drains. In other words, you might as well catch as much of the dirt as you can before it gets on the floor, rather than worry about getting it up after it gets there. In addition, a device such as this would help keep the air in the building cleaner.

JOAN SHINEW

A few weeks ago, when I set out to prepare myself for this discussion, the first thing I did was to arm myself with some good basic statistics. I went first to the man who heads our buildings and maintenance operation and then proceeded to the business manager's office.

When I returned to my own office to ponder all my facts and figures, I was dismayed to discover that they did not really add up. At this point I recalled a conversation I once had with a cataloger, when I found myself somewhat confused at the card catalog and inquired as to what the filing rule was in a particular instance. Her reply was to the effect that the rule did not matter; it just felt right to file that way, and that was how it was done. As I thought about our carpeting, I concluded that perhaps this was my best argument—it just feels right and that is why we like it and approve it.

I did come up, however, with a few facts about our installation. Our library is carpeted throughout except for a small processing room and a small front entranceway—altogether, about 40,000 square feet of carpeting. The carpet is 80 percent wool, 20 percent nylon, with a pile weight of approximately 16 ounces per square yard. The pile height is 1/8 inch, and it is woven on a cotton backing. A 3/16-inch, built-in, sponge rubber cushion is permanently fused to the floor side of the carpeting by a vulcanizing process.

We used beige tweed carpeting on the lower two floors, and burnt orange on the upper two floors. The orange is especially handsome in our second-floor atrium area, which opens to a skylight above and is furnished with upholstered chairs and lounges in tones of green and gold. You cannot please everyone all of the time in matters of colors, but I have concluded that we were able to please everyone part of the time with these two colors in our carpeting.

Right after we opened our building, I was constantly answering two questions. One was: This beige carpeting downstairs is just wonderful; why did you ever use that awful orange color upstairs? And, of course, the alternate question was: Oh, that orange carpeting upstairs is magnificent; why did you put this brown stuff downstairs? So if we could just route the right people to the right floor, we could keep everybody happy.

Unfortunately, the orange carpeting in our atrium area got off to a poor start. The building was barely open, and not really finished, when on a fine Sunday afternoon we had one of our more vigorous Colorado hailstorms and discovered that the rain gutters were inadequate to handle the hail. As the hail clogged the gutters, and the water backed up and poured through the skylight into the atrium area like Niagara Falls, just three sad people were

there as witnesses: the librarian emeritus, my predecessor, and myself. My predecessor, Ellsworth Mason, with his usual resourcefulness, began vacuuming up the two inches of sandy water that floated about. The atrium smelled very much like a wet collie dog for a couple of days, but the carpet survived far better than we had dared hope. Some water lines, however, still show, and shampooing just seems to bring them out more.

Now I want to talk briefly about why carpeting feels right in our building. First of all, we used it for aesthetic reasons. It provides a striking and softening contrast to the concrete columns throughout the building and to the ceiling which contains the lighting fixtures. In areas where we have upholstered lounge furniture, the color and the texture contrasts are all very pleasing. The carpeting affords a superb surface to walk on and seems to cut those fifty miles librarians walk each day almost in half. Another advantage is that it reduces noise levels to a remarkable degree. Combined with the drapes on the main floor, it is an excellent acoustical material. A normal speaking voice in the public areas does not carry at all.

For the most part, we like the effect that the carpet has on college students and faculty. It has made the building very inviting—a sharp contrast to the extremely dismal, uncomfortable, and colorless building we inhabited earlier. Now the library is a place where students and faculty enjoy spending their time. Soon after moving into the building we discovered that on beautiful Sunday afternoons, when no one really should be indoors, we had more than twice as many people in our building as the old building could accommodate at capacity.

Students tend to relax in the atmosphere created by carpeting. For the most part this is good. We do not permit them to bring food and drinks into the building, and this restriction helps to prevent the atmosphere from getting too casual. However, the students do not hesitate to sprawl comfortably on the carpet in the stack areas in order to poke and browse on the bottom shelf, and I think this is fine.

The head of our building and maintenance operation has become a strong proponent of carpeting as a floor covering and, as a result of having used it in this building, is using it more and more elsewhere on the campus. He tells me that he is now planning to use carpeting in the corridors of a new men's dormitory. He feels that it is difficult to gauge maintenance costs precisely, but he does believe that the carpeting represents a savings of one custodian in our building. We employ two custodians, and presumably, because of the relatively small amount of time necessary for maintaining the carpeting, these custodians are free for other tasks, such as vacuuming or dusting the books, et cetera. The maintenance head estimates that a custodian's salary over a period of ten years would actually pay for the carpeting. The business manager is quick to observe, however, that the library does not actually bank and save that money; it just hopes the saving goes into better and more extensive custodial service.

The very high traffic areas of carpet are vacuumed daily, but much of the stack areas need vacuuming only once in two weeks. Our custodians have a spot-cleaning kit for routine cleaning, and we do a thorough shampoo job once or twice a year. This is a building which has about 800 people coming and going daily.

The head of maintenance has strong feelings about color and points out to me that beige, gray, and dark tones are much easier to maintain, and he regrets the burnt orange color. Having reported this on his behalf, I confess that I cannot go along with his viewpoint. The orange has been very effective in our building, and I am inclined to think that the initial dousing which it received in the hailstorm I mentioned earlier is one of the reasons why it has not stayed so fresh-looking in the atrium area.

The head of maintenance is also an advocate of rubber backing, pointing out that it prevents dirt from filtering through and acting as an abrasive underneath the carpeting. It also allows no slipping, but holds firm. The one problem we have had is with the seams, which tend to pull apart. In discussing this problem we both felt that it was the result of a poor installation.

Static electricity has not been enough of a problem for us to take any action. It varies with climatic conditions and at this time of year is nonexistent. During our cold, dry, winter periods we have varying amounts of it—I believe it correlates particularly with the dryness—and some people observe it more than others. Personally I tend to be fairly oblivious of static, but I notice that visitors in the winter are often conscious of it. Our maintenance man says that we could use a spray on the carpet, but there is some evidence that this can act as an abrasive, and he is hesitant to do so unless the need is urgent.

We find that rubber-wheeled book trucks move very smoothly over our carpeting, and the stiletto heels which we ladies persist in wearing are no problem. All in all, we have been very pleased by our choice, and I think any change at this point would bring protests from the library staff, the maintenance staff, and—I strongly suspect—our library patrons.

Discussion

Question: Mr. Rawlinson has indicated that in a new installation we should buy a little more carpeting than the area requires, in order to be able to replace badly worn or soiled spots. Is there any rule of thumb as to whether one should buy 5 percent or 40 percent more?

MR. RAWLINSON: Actually, in our case, it was just luck. There was some left over, and we were very happy to have it.

Question: I would like to ask Mr. Johnston to elucidate. He said that self-polishing waxes do not require buffing. Is this really true and would he please give us the brand name of a self-polishing wax which is equal to what we have been putting on our floors for the last thirty-five years and buffing all this time?

MR. JOHNSTON: The new vinyl floor finishes (there are also vinyl waxes) do not require buffing and, in fact, will not take buffing. They are applied as a finish perhaps once or twice a year and are available from several manufacturers. We make one called Armstrong Polymeric Vinyl Finish. I think the Johnson Company makes a similar one. They are specifically used for vinyl surface materials.

Question: Can you put this material on a cork floor, too?

MR. JOHNSTON: No, a vinyl floor finish would not work very well on a cork floor. You have to use a buffable wax on cork. Vinyl on vinyl is the answer.

Question: With what flooring material do members of the panel compare the carpet they now use, and what is the expected life of carpets that they use?

MR. RAWLINSON: One of the results we are all waiting to see is the life of a complete wall-to-wall carpet installation. That is the reason why I wish there were figures extant as to how long it lasted in the earlier installation at our university. Frankly, we do not know. We have had five, almost six, years with the carpeting now, and we see no indication that its duration will be so short as to embarrass us or to be a problem. As far as we can tell, it is going to last as long as the harder types of floor coverings.

MR. FLETCHER: In our investigation we heard of one department store that had used an all-wool, commercial carpet for about fifteen years. We expect a five to seven years' life under heavy traffic conditions and better than ten years' for other areas.

Question: I would like to ask about the laying of carpet in stack areas. Do you put down the carpet, then put the stacks on top; or do you just lay the carpet along the aisles?

MR. FLETCHER: In regard to our carpet, all the hair pads were fastened with a tack strip; the carpet does not move. The stacks are free-standing on the carpet.

MR. RAWLINSON: In the case of the undergraduate library, the entire floor area was covered with carpet; then the stacks and furniture were placed on top of the carpet.

MISS SHINEW: In our case the procedure was different. The stacks were standing, and the carpet was placed around the stack area.